ILLUMINATION
Lighting the Way to College Composition

ANN LEWIS

MARCI SELVA

Sacramento City College

KENDALL/HUNT PUBLISHING COMPANY
4050 Westmark Drive   Dubuque, Iowa 52002

Contents

PART I: THE RHETORIC

PART II: THE READER

CHAPTER 4:   Narration and Description   51

CHAPTER 5:   Exemplification   73

CHAPTER 6: Comparison and Contrast 93

CHAPTER 7: Definition 117

CHAPTER 8: Argument and Persuasion 139

PART III: THE HANDBOOK

CHAPTER 9: The Basics: Parts of Speech 159

Preface

We have designed *Illumination: Lighting the Way to College Composition* to be used in higher-level developmental writing courses or basic freshman composition courses that do not have a research component. This all-in-one text contains the following:

- A straightforward Rhetoric
- An accessible Handbook
- A comprehensive Reader that includes multi-cultural selections that vary in complexity

Working with beginning college writers as coordinators of Sacramento City College's pre-college composition program—particularly the departmental final exam—we have come to realize that these students need a textbook designed with them in mind, and that such a textbook should include

- all the materials a student will need in one text,
- clear, concise, and readable language,
- information displayed in a student-friendly format, and
- essays that not only engage the students as readers but also provide them with models and ideas for their own writing.

This book is especially useful in courses where students are required to take a departmental final exam—or midterm—that requires response to, analysis of, and incorporation of examples from a secondary source.

We have also designed this textbook to be a teaching "tool," formulating our discussion questions, exercises, and guidelines for writing to complement the instructor's lesson plans.

ACKNOWLEDGMENTS

This book would not have been completed without the invaluable assistance of our editors, Mona Jo Dobson and Lynne Koester. Also, we are very grateful for the advice, input, and feedback provided by Lynne Koester, particularly on the Handbook section. Additionally, we would like to thank our Dean, Julia Jolly, and our colleagues in the Language and Literature Division at Sacramento City College, who have supported and encouraged us throughout. Finally, we would like to add a special thanks to the students of Sacramento City College for everything *they* have taught *us*.

Marci Selva would also like to thank . . .

- My co-author, Ann Lewis, for being a wonderful friend and colleague and for reminding me always to keep a sense of humor;
- My friends, whose love and support I carry with me wherever I go;
- And, most of all, my family—Carol, Norman, and Michelle Selva, for far more things than I can possibly list here. *Mille grazie, mia famiglia.*

Ann Lewis would also like to thank . . .

- Marci—an exceptional co-author, friend, and colleague
- My American family—Lynne, Andrea, Stephanie
- My Australian family—Roslyn, Michelle, Brett, and Daniel
- My son Tim—who helps me span the Pacific

PART 1
THE RHETORIC

CHAPTER 1
The Essay

COMPONENTS OF THE ESSAY

Throughout this book, we will be discussing essays: how to write them, how to read them, how to analyze them, how to respond to them. So perhaps we should begin by establishing exactly what an essay is. An essay should contain several essential components:

- The *introduction* does exactly what its name implies; it "introduces" the essay topic to the reader, giving the reader a brief overview of the subject. Since it is the first part of the essay the reader will read, it should be clear, relevant, and interesting. Generally, the *thesis* should be included in the introduction.

- The *thesis* is perhaps the most important part of the essay. Also called the "main idea," the thesis is a clear, concise statement of what the writer intends to prove or illustrate in the essay. The thesis is usually just one sentence, but in more sophisticated essays it may be longer. The thesis is not merely a statement telling the writer what the essay will be about; it includes the *general topic* of the essay AND the *main idea* that the writer wishes to convey about the topic.

Example:

    (GENERAL TOPIC)   (MAIN IDEA)
Requiring public school students to wear uniforms <u>undermines their freedom and infringes upon their civil liberties</u>.

- The *body* of the essay is the part of the essay that supports the thesis. The body is made up of a number of focused, well-developed *paragraphs,* each of which should include the following:

  - *A topic sentence:* Similar to the thesis, a topic sentence presents the reader with the "main idea" of a particular paragraph and provides a focus for the paragraph. A good paragraph will always have a topic sentence.

- **Support:** The support (or "evidence") is the material a writer uses to illustrate and prove his or her points. The support in an essay may consist of factual information, statistics, real-life and/or hypothetical examples, definitions, well-reasoned opinions, or a combination of some or all of these.

- The *conclusion* is not just the "end" of the essay, but a concluding paragraph in which the writer leaves the reader with something to think about, whether it be an important question, a realization the writer has come to, or a reflection on the significance of the topic. Try to avoid, whenever possible, making the conclusion a mere summary of the points covered in the essay.

The following diagram may help you visualize the structure of an essay:

FORMAT FOR ESSAY PLANNING

Introduction:

Thesis:_____

_____

_____

Body Paragraph #1:

   *Topic Sentence:*_____

_____

_____

   Supporting Details:

Body Paragraph #2:

   *Topic Sentence:*_____

_____

_____

Supporting Details:

Body Paragraph #3:

   *Topic Sentence:*_____

_____

_____

   Supporting Details:

Body Paragraph #4:

   *Topic Sentence:*_____

_____

_____

   Supporting Details:

Conclusion:

**Note: Your essay need not be limited to four paragraphs.

INTRODUCTION AND THESIS

The Thesis

We have already established that a thesis sentence conveys to the reader the main/ controlling idea of the essay. Now we should get more specific and explain what a good thesis does and does not do.

First, a good thesis sentence does not

ASK A QUESTION

- Why do people spend thousands of dollars a year on gym memberships, weight loss programs, and diet drugs?
- Why do people go to health clubs?

STATE A FACT

- Last year, 1 in 4 people in the greater Sacramento area belonged to a gym.
- In America, more and more people are joining gyms.
- Many people join weight loss programs and take diet drugs.

PROVIDE A TITLE

- Our obsession with "health."
- America's health club craze.
- We Americans and our diet drugs.

MAKE AN ANNOUNCEMENT

- In this essay, I am going to discuss people who join health clubs.
- In this essay, I am going to talk about how many people join gyms and spend their money on weight loss programs, and I will suggest some reasons why people do this.

CONTAIN WISHY WASHY phrases such as

- I think
- I believe
- I feel
- It seems to me

SET UP A 5-PARAGRAPH ESSAY

- Americans spend thousands of dollars a year on gym memberships, weight loss programs, and diet drugs to look better, to feel better, and to be accepted by their peers.

Instead, a good thesis sentence

- Addresses the assignment prompt
- Identifies the general topic and writer's opinion about the topic
- Is worthy of development
- Presents a debatable claim
- Is narrow enough to be developed in the number of pages specified by the assignment directions.
- Is not so narrow that the ideas cannot be developed
- Is clearly stated in concrete language

Here are some examples of good thesis sentences:

- Because of the recent surge in health club memberships for people aged 55 plus, many gyms will probably have to begin modifying some of their equipment and/or programs offered.
- Americans spend millions of dollars a year on gym memberships, weight loss programs, and diet drugs not because they are concerned about being healthy, but because they are concerned about being accepted by society.
- With approximately half of all adult Americans now classified as being overweight, health clubs may need to offer more incentives to encourage new memberships and motivate members to attend.

EXERCISE 1A

Revising Thesis Sentences

DIRECTIONS: Each of the following thesis sentences needs revision. Using the guidelines discussed above, revise each thesis so that it communicates in a clear and effective manner.

1. I think that people judge other people unfairly based on clothing styles, and that's not fair.
2. In my essay, I will explore the various reasons why smoking on campus should be prohibited.
3. Violence in today's society.
4. Each year, drunk driving contributes to thousands of deaths on our nation's roadways.
5. Do you think that we can decrease violent crime and drug addiction in our society by making drugs legal?
6. When selecting a roommate, you should find out a lot of information about the person before allowing him/her to move in, such as credit history, employment, and what kinds of people he or she hangs around with.
7. Kids and the epidemic of television violence.
8. Should the death penalty be abolished?
9. This essay will provide different definitions of the concept of beauty.
10. I want to talk about the traffic problem in Sacramento.

The Introduction

Because your opening paragraph is the reader's introduction to your essay, you should spend considerable time crafting one that engages the reader's attention and compels him or her to continue reading. There are various techniques you can use to capture the reader's interest:

Technique	Effect on the Reader
Anecdote (Story)	We all enjoy stories and an anecdote will entertain and draw your reader into the essay.
Question(s)	Whenever we hear a question, we feel compelled to answer it. Your reader will want to continue reading the essay to learn the answer(s).
Statistics/Facts	Using statistics and/or facts will establish you as a knowledgeable person on the subject and help establish your credibility as a writer.
Definition	Providing a definition in your introduction will help clarify unfamiliar words or concepts and establish a clearer focus for your thesis.
Quotations	Like the use of statistics, your use of quotations will help establish your credibility and knowledge about your subject, particularly if the quotation is from a reputable source. This type of introduction is particularly useful for essays that respond to sources.

Sample Student Introductions

Anecdote

While riding the stationary bike at my local gym the other day, I observed my fellow gym-goers and came to a startling conclusion: none of them looked happy. That's right. As I rode, I surveyed the aerobic floor, the weight machines, and the cardio area, and while I noticed a great deal of concentration, a lot of sweat, and many color-coordinated spandex outfits, I saw not a single smile, not so much as a flicker of contentment, on any of the faces of those around me. I was stunned. As I continued to pedal and sweat on the road to nowhere, I suddenly realized that my motivation for exercising is not to achieve better health and a better quality of life. On the contrary, it's about nearly everything *but* health: that great pair of pants in the store window that I want to be able to wear; my upcoming high school reunion; my thinner friends who look better in a bathing suit than I do; the women's magazine on my coffee table that shows what I'll look like if I only exercise hard enough and long enough. It was there, on the stationary bike at the gym, that I realized why so many people were exercising and not enjoying it: Americans spend millions of dollars a year on gym memberships, weight loss programs, and diet drugs not because they are concerned about being healthy, but because they are concerned about being accepted by society.

Questions

While at the gym the other day, I saw not a single smile, not so much as a flicker of contentment, on any of the faces of those around me. Could it be that people don't actually *enjoy* exercise? And if this is indeed the case, why do so many of us frequent health clubs on a regular basis? Why do we expend time, money, and energy if we aren't enjoying ourselves in the process? Perhaps in order to answer these questions, we should examine our own individual reasons for working out. It's good for our heart, right? It helps alleviate stress, right? It builds strong muscles and helps reduce the risk of disease, right? Wrong. The truth is far less noble and somewhat disturbing. In fact, Americans spend millions of dollars a year on gym memberships, weight loss programs, and diet drugs not because they are concerned about being healthy, but because they are concerned about being accepted by society.

Statistics

Statistics show that 64 percent of people who join a health club attend faithfully for the first two months of membership, only to quit going altogether at the end of that two-month period. This statistic is surprising in itself, but what is even more alarming is the amount of money spent on these memberships that, ultimately, goes to waste. The average health club membership costs approximately $40 per month and often requires new members pay for a year's membership in advance. Thus, a member who joins a club and then "drops out" after only two months has squandered approximately $400 in unused health club dues. Given these disturbing facts, health clubs need to look for ways to motivate members to exercise regularly, thus ensuring that their money will not be wasted.

Definition

The American Heritage Dictionary defines "health" as "a soundness, especially of body or mind; a condition of well-being." This "soundness" or "well-being" may be achieved through a variety of means, one of which is maintaining overall physical fitness. Over the past two decades, the number of gyms (and, accordingly, gym members) has increased dramatically, as have the numbers of at-home fitness products, including exercise equipment and videos, and diet plans. On the surface, this unprecedented interest in physical fitness may seem like a positive sign that Americans are sincerely invested in their health; however, this interest takes on more negative undertones when we consider another, more unsettling trend: the dramatic increase in unrealistic media portrayals of the "perfect body" and a corresponding increase in the number of Americans, both women and men, who suffer from eating disorders and other body image-related mental and physical health issues. Despite recent protests against the media's promotion of an unrealistic body ideal, Americans continue to put their bodies and lives at risk (and spend millions of dollars a year in the process) with excessive exercise, so-called "miracle diets," and diet pills and supplements promising fast results. Clearly, many of the drastic measures that Americans are currently taking to stay in shape run counter to the whole notion of health, the idea of "soundness" or "well-being." Why, then, the enormous expenditure of time and money? And what compels people to put their health at risk in the name of "fitness"? The answer is simple, yet disturbing: Americans spend millions of dollars each year on gym memberships, weight-loss programs, and diet drugs, not because they are concerned about being healthy, but because they are concerned about being accepted by society.

Quotation(s)

Health clubs, once the exclusive domain of young people, now seem to be assuming a different role. In "Baby Boomers Turn into Die-Hard Athletes to Cheat Aging and Death," published in the *Chicago Tribune,* Lola Small-wood points out that people over the age of 55 now constitutes "the largest percentage of health club members." What should health clubs do to accommodate this more mature clientele? Will these new members want to participate in fast-paced aerobic workouts, heavy weightlifting, and/or trendy dance classes? Or will they be more drawn to lower-impact, less strenuous exercise such as walking and water aerobics? Because of the recent surge in health club memberships for people aged 55 plus, many gyms will probably have to begin modifying some of their equipment and/or programs offered to ensure that members of all ages can benefit from their health club memberships.

BODY PARAGRAPHS

Once you have introduced your topic and established the focus of your essay, your next task is to provide adequate support for your thesis. This support should be presented in several body paragraphs, each having its own main idea and supporting details. In composing body paragraphs, it's a good idea to think of each paragraph as a sort of "mini-essay," with the main idea of the paragraph stated in a clear, focused topic sentence. Each paragraph should cover one main point and should remain focused on that particular point throughout. This means that all supporting details should be relevant to the main idea stated in your topic sentence.

The Topic Sentence

The topic sentence helps focus your paragraph in the same way that a thesis sentence helps focus your essay. Many of the criteria for writing a good thesis sentence also apply to the topic sentence. For instance, a good topic sentence should not state a fact, make an announcement, or contain wishy-washy phrases. Neither should it be too broad to develop in one paragraph nor so narrow that there is nothing else to say. Instead, a good topic sentence should

- Provide focus for the paragraph
- Support the thesis
- Contain a topic and an opinion about the topic

|——————— TOPIC ——————| OPINION

An appreciation for the simple things can help us to lead happier, more contented lives.

|– OPINION –| TOPIC

It is essential that students in their first semester of college be taught not only how to be good college students, but how NOT to be bad college students as well.

|——————— TOPIC ——————| OPINION

In order to win the next Super Bowl, the Oakland Raiders will also have to make some changes to their lineup.

- Often, you will not think about your topic sentences as you write your first draft; you may just want to get your ideas down as quickly as you can. As you write you may already know how each paragraph supports your thesis, but remember that the reader does not necessarily share this knowledge with you. When you revise your essay, add topic sentences to clarify the connections.

- Often it seems "easier" to write without using topic sentences, but there is one big advantage to including them: Even if you do not state your ideas as clearly and completely as you would like, topic sentences will AT LEAST let your reader know what you are trying to say and she/he will be able to follow your train of thought.

EXERCISE 1B

Writing Topic Sentences

DIRECTIONS: Write topic sentences for the following topics:

1. Saving money
2. Why student fees should not be increased
3. Working while attending college
4. Why we should recycle
5. Public transport vs. driving

Types of Support

Once you have devised your topic sentence, you need to support it with sufficient and relevant evidence. Here are some types of support you can use:

Support	Advantages
Examples (see "Exemplification")	make abstract ideas more concrete.
Facts/statistics (see "Argumentation")	establish credibility and show the reader that you are familiar with the topic.
Names	will bring real people into your writing.
Sensory Details (see "Narration/Description")	will appeal to the reader's five senses.

Paragraph Organization

Of course, one good way to make sure your reader follows your thoughts is to give careful consideration to the way you organize your ideas. As you become a more experienced writer, you should experiment with different methods of presentation. On a very basic level, here are two diagrams:

DIAGRAM #1

Topic Sentence: _____

Support/Example: _____

_____

Support/Example: _____

_____

_____

Support/Example: _____

_____

_____

Support/Example: _____

_____

_____

Support/Example: _____

_____

_____

Concluding Sentence (optional) _____

Example:

A passenger list of the early years of the Orient Express would read like a *Who's Who of the World,* from art to politics. Sarah Bernhardt and her Italian counterpart Eleonora Duse used the train to thrill the stages of Europe. For musicians, there were Toscanini and Mahler. Dancers Nijinsky and Pavlova were there, while lesser performers like Harry Houdini and the girls of the Ziegfeld Follies also rode the rails. Violinists were allowed to practice on the train, and occasionally one might see trapeze artists hanging like bats from the baggage racks.

—Barnaby Conrad III, "Train of Kings"

DIAGRAM # 2

Topic Sentence: _____

_____

Supporting Point: _____

_____

Details: _____

_____

Supporting Point: _____

_____

Details: _____

_____

Supporting Point: _____

_____

Details: _____

_____

Concluding Sentence (optional): _____

_____

Example:

How (Not) to Be a College Student

It is essential that students in their first semester of college be taught not only how to be good college students, but how NOT to be bad college students as well. One "don't" that all students should be taught is "don't let your social life interfere with your studies." Many new college students, feeling liberated from the constraints of living at home and attending high school, extend their weekend activities (i.e., "partying") onto the week nights as well, going out every night instead of doing homework and getting a good night's sleep. Often, this results in the students falling behind in their classes and sometimes not showing up to class at all. Another big "don't" that college students need to be aware of is "don't pass up opportunities for extra help." Most colleges offer a variety of free services, including one-on-one tutoring, study groups, and special centers (often called "labs") to help students master the skills necessary to pass their classes. Students who are having difficulty in their classes and fail to take advantage of these opportunities may find themselves hoping for a miracle at final exam time; sadly, for most, this miracle never occurs. The last and most important "don't" that all college students must be aware of is "don't treat college as if it were an extension of high school." Many students, having gotten used to getting away with certain attitudes and behaviors in high school, might find themselves in shock when a college professor refuses to accept a late assignment or reprimands them for talking in class. Students who are unaware of the vast differences between high school and college may find themselves in shock when the results of their behavior (i.e. bad grades and a bad relationship with their professors) become apparent. Clearly, it is not enough for students to simply be academically prepared for college; they must be taught the discipline and maturity necessary to succeed in higher education as well.

Other Organizational Strategies

Here are some other organizational strategies to consider:

Chronological Order—Time Order

I labored with excitement that first morning—and all the days after. The work was harder than I could have expected. But it was never as tedious as my friends had warned me it would be. There was too much physical pleasure in the labor. Especially early in the day, I would be most alert to the sensations of movement and straining. Beginning around seven each morning (when the air was still damp but the scent of weeds and dry earth anticipated the heat of the sun), I would feel my body resist the first thrusts of the shovel. My arms, tightened by sleep, would gradually loosen; after only several minutes, sweat would gather in beads on my forehead and then—a short while later—I would feel my chest silky with sweat in the breeze. I would return to my work: A nervous spark of pain would fly up my arm and settle to burn like an amber in the thick of my shoulder An hour, two passed. Three. My whole body would assume regular movements; my shoveling would be described by identical, even movements. Even later in the day, my enthusiasm for primitive sensation would survive the heat and the dust and the insects pricking my back. I would strain wildly for sensation as the day came to a close. At three-thirty, quitting time, I would stand upright and slowly let my head fall back, luxuriating in the feel of tightness relieved.

From "Workers" by Richard Rodriguez

Order of Importance – End With Your MOST Important Point/Example

At the beginning of the trans-Pacific journey, the floor and seats of the aircraft are freshly cleaned, the blankets and pillows neatly folded to greet the eager passengers, the headsets still hermetically sealed in their plastic pouches, and the "lavatories" are freshly-scrubbed and welcoming. However, after 10 hours, the aircraft has undergone a dramatic transformation. First, the headsets—many no longer intact—are now dangling from seat pockets, armrests, shoes, overhead bins, and other locations. Pillows—now the worse for wear—are wedged in various unseemly places: underfoot, under seats, and under the rear ends of passengers. The carpet is now almost invisible under layers of trash, including napkins, food wrappers, discarded magazines, shoes and socks, items of clothing, remnants of last night's dinner, and beverage cans. But, perhaps the most significant change has occured in the "lavatories." The waste receptacles are overflowing onto the floor, the counter and floor are wet, and the sink is clogged and/or coated with unidentifiable substances. But the worst change is that the sweet, clean smell of 10 hours ago has now been replaced by an accumulation of odors that blend together to create a noxious gas that floods the cabin when the door is opened. By this time, the passengers are still eager—to disembark.

Spatial – Where Do Things Appear in Relation to Other Things

But when the sick feeling goes away and I open my eyes, the red sweater's still sitting there like a big red mountain. I move the red sweater to the corner of my desk with my ruler. I move my pencil and books and eraser as far from it as possible. I even move my chair a little to the right. Not mine, not mine, not mine.

From "Eleven" by Sandra Cisneros

EXERCISE 1C

Paragraph Organization

DIRECTIONS: Using the tools discussed in this section, examine the following paragraph. Identify the following: 1) the topic sentence; 2) the method of organization.

Everyday Things

As our society becomes increasingly fast-paced, it is essential that we take a few moments every day to pause and appreciate the world around us, as this appreciation for the simple things can help us to lead happier, more contented lives. The most important things we overlook, and those we should pay more attention to, are those things found only in nature. For instance, the changing of the leaves in mid-fall is an extraordinary event. One tree can have several different colors of leaves – red, yellow, and orange – all at once. The same holds true for the sunsets in late summer and early fall that paint the sky in a dazzling array of hues, creating pictures far more beautiful than any that can be found in a museum. An awareness and appreciation of this beauty can lead us to appreciate the simply beauty of life itself, a life that exists away from busy freeways, crowded streets, and stressful work environments. Moreover, the animals that are all around us every day are another source of contentment and happiness that we often take for granted because of our busy lives. Whether it's watching the ground squirrels frolicking in the park or cuddling a beloved pet, animals have a proven therapeutic value; studies have shown that those who interact with animals on a regular basis have less stress and anxiety and hence live longer, happier lives. Lastly, and perhaps most importantly, we must pause every day, several times a day, and take in several deep breaths of fresh air. Air is the very essence of life, and it is in abundant supply wherever we go. Deep breathing has been proven to reduce stress and stress-related conditions including anxiety, headaches, and mood swings. The best things in life are truly free, and they can benefit us in many ways if we are willing to slow down the pace of our lives and take advantage of what nature has to offer.

Coherence

It is not enough to organize and develop your ideas; if you don't tie the ideas together, they will seem like a list and your paragraph will sound choppy. For example:

> I woke up. I got out of bed. I had coffee. I showered. I got dressed. I went to school. I attended my classes. I had lunch. I went to work. I got home; I did my homework. I had dinner. I went to bed.

You must show the relationship(s) between your ideas and your ideas must "flow" smoothly from one sentence to the next. Here are some techniques that will help.

- **Deliberate and Selective Repetition of Key Words and Phrases:**
  - The rising cost of a college education is a significant problem for college **students.** Consequently, many **students** may decide to drop out of school.
  - The American River Bike **Trail** extends from Discovery Park to Folsom Lake. On any given day, dozens of health-conscious people flock to this **trail** to exercise.

- **Synonyms**
  - The big bad wolf lay in wait for Little Red Riding Hood as she walked to her grandmother's **house.** The **dwelling** was located deep in the forest.

- **Pronouns**
  - **George W. Bush, Bill Clinton, and Ronald Reagan** were all former governors of their respective states. **They** also brought their dogs to the White House.

- **Transitions and Transitional Phrases:**
Because all writing has an audience, **clarity** is of the utmost importance. One of the ways that you can add clarity to your writing is through the use of **transitions** and **transitional phrases,** words or phrases which alert readers to **relationships** between ideas and paragraphs and **emphasize** the purpose of your writing. In using transitions and transitional phrases, you must first determine what type of relationship you are trying to show or what you want to emphasize. Transitions and transitional phrases are used

  - **To indicate time and sequence:** *next, later, after, while, meanwhile, first, second, third (firstly, secondly, thirdly), shortly, thereafter, subsequently, soon, at that time, finally, last (lastly).*
    When I arrived home from work, my front door was unlocked. **Later,** I noticed that my stereo and some of my jewelry were missing, so I called the police. **Shortly,** a police car arrived at my house.

  - **To signal addition of a point or idea:** *in addition, additionally, also, moreover, further, furthermore, and, besides, next, too, first, second, etc.*
    My new laptop is much faster than my old one; **additionally,** it has many new features.

  - **To signal a comparison:** *likewise, similarly, also, again, in the same manner, in comparison.*
    Frank has difficulty getting to class on time. **Likewise,** he is often late for work.

  - **To signal a contrast:** *in contrast, on the other hand, however, although, even though, still, yet, but, nevertheless, conversely, at the same time, regardless, despite, in spite of.*
    - **Although** life can be difficult, I still find it enjoyable.
    - The college recently created 150 new parking spaces; **nevertheless,** finding parking on campus is still a problem.

  - **To signal an upcoming example:** *for example, for instance, such as, specifically, thus, to illustrate, namely, in particular, in fact.*
    Smoking is damaging to the body in many ways. **For example,** it contributes to premature aging, lung cancer, and heart disease, among other things.

  - **To signal a cause-effect relationship:** *as a result, consequently, since, accordingly, if . . . then, for this reason, as a consequence of, so, therefore, thus.*
    - The fog rolled in early this morning; **consequently,** the commute on the freeway was a disaster.
    - **Since** you refuse to listen to my advice, you will have to learn the hard way.

- **To signal a conclusion or a summary of ideas presented:** *In conclusion, in summary, finally, thus, in short, it is evident that.*
  In conclusion, it is essential to conduct extensive research before purchasing a used car.

- **To signal a concession:** *Granted, certainly, while it is true that.*
  Granted, parking on campus is a problem; however, it is not an excuse for tardiness.

EXERCISE 1D

Using Transitions

DIRECTIONS: From the above list, choose transitions or transitional phrases which best emphasize the relationships between the ideas presented, and insert the transitions into the paragraph where there are spaces. Use the suggestions in parentheses as a guide.

Yesterday, a curious thing happened that taught me an important lesson about thinking before I act. I was out for a walk in my neighborhood, when I saw a man standing on the street near a parked car, behaving in a manner that I found strange. _____ (time/sequence), he walked around the outside of the car, looking at it as if he were surveying it from all angles. _____ (time/sequence), he got down on the pavement and began peering underneath the car. This seemed a little odd to me, so I stopped at a distance and stood watching him to see what else he would do. _____ (time/sequence), he got up off the ground and pressed his face against the window, peering inside the car. Needless to say, I was becoming a bit concerned. He was spending a great deal of time looking at this car, and it appeared he was trying to find a way to get in it. _____ (addition), his appearance caused me some alarm; he wasn't wearing any shoes, and he appeared to be wearing pajamas. _____ (addition), he was exhibiting other suspicious behavior. _____ (example), the whole time he was looking at the car, he was shaking his head, and I think I heard him cursing. _____ (concession), you see a lot of strange things in this town, but this was starting to worry me; _____ (cause-effect), I did what I thought any concerned citizen would do. Keeping my distance, I got on my cell phone and called the police. _____ (time/sequence), a squad car arrived and pulled up alongside the vehicle. The officers got out and began speaking to the man, gesturing toward me, cowering under a nearby tree. The man responded, gesturing toward the car. _____ (time/sequence), I stood there wondering what was going on. The man seemed a bit agitated. _____ (contrast), the officers seemed to be laughing as if the situation were amusing. _____ (time/sequence), one of the policemen called out to me, asking me to come over to where the three of them were. As I approached them, I heard the man say, "I guess that'll teach me a lesson." The policemen explained to me that the man was the owner of the car. He had come outside in his pajamas to get his brief-case out of the car and had proceeded to lock the keys inside the car. _____ (cause-effect), he was not only locked out of his car, but out of his apartment as well—the key to his complex's security gate was on his key ring. He had been looking at the car to see if he could figure out any way to get into it without breaking a window. _____ (addition or time/sequence), the reason he had been on the ground was that he thought he had a spare key hidden under the fender, but it wasn't there. He had as-sured the officers that if they helped him get into the car, he would go in-side his apartment and get his driver's license to prove that he was the owner of the car. Needless to say, I felt like a jerk. I had nearly gotten some-one arrested for trying to get into his own car. _____ (conclusion/sum-mary), I learned an important lesson that day about finding out the truth before jumping to conclusions. If I had just approached the man and asked him if he needed help, I would have learned that he wasn't a car thief, and the police wouldn't have gotten involved.

CONCLUSION

Most of the techniques discussed in the "Introductions" section of this chapter can also be used in writing conclusions. Remember, your conclu-sion should be more than just a re-statement of the points you have made in your essay; it should provide a satisfying end to the essay and leave your reader with something significant to ponder. The conclusion should help your reader to come away from reading your essay with a deeper un-derstanding of the issue(s) you have discussed and perhaps an interest in learning more about your topic.

Some examples of effective conclusions:

Only recently do I realize my error. I wish I could have been the one to say, on that first fall afternoon, "Tiffany's not ugly, fat, or stinky. She's just like you and me, and we're all here together." Really, I wish anyone would have said it. I know now that people need each other, and I wish I could tell the fourth grade that we could all be friends, that we could help each other with our problems. I wish that I could go back. But all I can do is apologize. So Tiffany, for all my shortcomings, and for sacrificing you for the sake of belonging, please forgive me.

From "Tiffany Stephenson: An Apology" by Bjorn Skogquist

For the ancient Greeks, drama taught and reinforced compassion within a society. The object of Greek tragedy was to inspire empathy in the audience so that the common response to the hero's fall was: "There, but for the grace of God, go I." Could it be that this was the response of the mother who offered the dollar, the French woman who gave the food? Could it be that the homeless, like those an-cients, are reminding us of our common humanity? Of course, there is a differ-ence. This play doesn't end—and the players can't go home.

From "On Compassion" by Barbara Lazear Ascher

CHAPTER 2

The Writing Process

BEFORE YOU BEGIN WRITING: PRE-WRITING STRATEGIES

Think about the last time you took a quiz or test in one of your classes. Chances are, your teacher informed you of the date of the test and the material to be covered on the test in advance, in order to give you adequate time to prepare. There is a good chance too, that you studied, at least a little bit, to become familiar with the material and to prepare for questions you might be asked. What would happen if you didn't study? Would you be able to simply walk into the testing room on the day of the test, sit down, pick up your pencil and magically provide all the right answers? Probably not. Writing an essay is a lot like preparing for a test in several ways. One, you're usually given the writing assignment well in advance of the due date. Also, your teacher most likely goes over the assignment with you, making his or her expectations clear. And, writing an essay, like studying for and taking a test, is a **process.** A good essay does not just magically appear on the page without adequate preparation, just as the right answers on a test do not magically appear if you haven't studied. The writing process begins the minute your teacher hands you the essay assignment, and it does not end until you've made your final revisions, and you have carefully proofread and edited your writing.

The first step in the writing process is **pre-writing.** Remember that the prefix "pre" means "before," so you should think of pre-writing as what you do "before writing." This first step is where you take the assignment and "think" about the topic on paper; basically, it's just a way of getting your ideas out onto paper to see what you think about the topic and begin to organize your thoughts into a draft. Your pre-writing need not be perfectly organized or impeccably presented; it is by no means a finished product. It will undergo many changes and many additions and omissions on its way to becoming your first draft. On the following pages, you will find explanations of pre-writing methods, along with examples. At the beginning of your writing process, you should choose the method that works best for you.

Methods of Pre-writing

Brainstorming

The term *brainstorming* is just another way of saying *thinking*. Before you can begin to put pen to paper, you must first carefully read—and re-read—the assignment and think about what you are being asked to do. Next, you will have to think about possible topics and ways to approach these topics.

Freewriting

Freewriting is exactly what its name indicates; it's a method of pre-writing in which you simply write freely on the topic of your essay for a certain amount of time. First, decide the amount of time you want to spend freewriting, say 5-10 minutes, for example. You may want to set a timer to keep track of your time. Try to write continuously for the allotted time, and try to keep your pen or pencil in contact with the paper at all times. Do not worry about spelling, punctuation or grammar, and do not worry if you can't think of what to say; if necessary, keep writing "I don't know what to write" until you can think of something.

Example:

Topic: America's Fitness Craze

the topic is america's fitness craze what should I write? I exercize a little bit every day sometimes I go for walks or ride my bike in bad weather i go to the gym. Exercize can be fun sometimes but its not fun when you feel tired or when you wish you could be doing something else like playing a video game or using the computer. Sometimes I can't motivate myself to exercize and I feel guilty but. . .cant think of what to say. . .its ok to not exercize every day. Americans seem to be obsessed with exerciseing – I'm not sure why. Everybody seems to be so afraid of being fat –why? I think ads and media have a lot to do w/it because they show only really thin people who are in shape and it leads people to believe that they have to look like that too – I know I pay too much attention to what people look like on tv or in magazines – nobody's perfect, not even the people on tv. They just have people to dress them and put makeup on them and touch up their photos to make them look better – that's not real. . .hope I'm not getting off the topic here. . .I think exercize is really good as long as you don't overdo it or expect too much from it. People need to exercise for health first and not to look like a model because they'll be disappointed if they don't achieve the perfect body. . .drs. should advise people to exercise for good health and not emphasize looks too much. . .that way people will maybe start exercising for the right reasons

Listing

Listing is simply making a list of points about the assigned topic. Your list will most likely consist of words and ideas associated with the topic, as well as your own opinions about the topic and points from your own observations and experiences. As with freewriting, don't worry about punctuation, spelling, or sentence structure in your list. The key is to get your ideas onto the paper to give you something to work from when writing your first draft.

Example:

Topic: America's Obsession With Fitness

Gyms everywhere
Rise in gym memberships
Personal training = $$$$$$
Eating disorders (anorexia, bulimia, etc.)
Business people in running shoes at lunchtime
Paradox – increase in obese Americans?
Media images= guilt and shame = more exercise
Unrealistic expectations
"ideal body" –what is it?
Health or vanity?
Gyms always packed
Info-mercials (exercise machines, diet pills, etc.)
Fad diets = billion dollar business

Outlining

In previous writing classes you have taken, you may have been taught to make a formal outline when planning assignments. For some students, this method of pre-writing works well because it provides a clear method of organizing their ideas. Though the outline is a bit more formal than either freewriting or listing, it should still be considered a form of pre-writing; therefore, you should avoid getting bogged down at this stage with spelling, punctuation, and sentence structure.

Example:

Topic: America's Obsession with Fitness

I. Causes of Obsession
   A. Advertising and other media promote fitness as path to social acceptance
   B. Medical establishment warns (threatens?) regarding obesity-mortality connection
   C. Companies play on vanity of consumers to make $$$$
   D. Reports of drastic increase in obesity rates in U.S

II. Backlash/Consequences
   A. Americans spending millions of $$ on gym memberships, equipment, diets
   B. Increase in eating disorders

    C. Increase in exercise-related injuries
    D. Unrealistic expectations = pressure, guilt, feelings of failure

III. My Experience
    A. Gym member for six years
    B. Influenced by media – "thin is in"
    C. Intense pressure to exercise for appearance reasons
    D. Never satisfied with "results"

IV. Solutions
    A. Media should show more realistic body types
    B. Gyms should emphasize sensible workouts and nutrition
    C. Doctors should provide more info to patients on exercising for health reasons, not just for appearance

**Whether or not you write your essay using an outline, any reader should EASILY be able to make an outline of your finished essay.

Clustering

Clustering is a more "creative" form of pre-writing in which you place ideas in "clusters" to create a more visual organization of your ideas. For many students, clustering is helpful because it allows you to "see" the connections between your ideas.

Example:

Topic: America's Obsession With Fitness

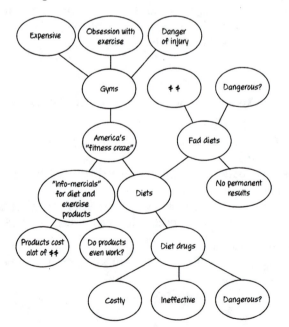

NOW IT'S TIME TO BEGIN WRITING: PREPARING A DRAFT

Armed with all of the ideas you came up with in the pre-writing process, it is now time to sit down at the computer and write a draft. As you write your essay, try not to "obsess" about grammar, punctuation, etc. Instead, try to get your essay written from start to finish so that you will have a draft to revise. **ALL** good writers plan on revising their work—usually several times. Below is a rough draft on the topic of fitness using the information gleaned in the pre-writing section.

Rough Draft: "America's Obsession With Fitness"

Nowadays, it seem's that American's are obsessed with fitness, especially with achieving the "ideal" body. Millions of American's go to gyms, take diet pills and other drugs and go on fad diets every day. Why do they do this, and do these things really give people what they are looking for? What are the consequences of America's obsession with fitness? This essay will explore the various ways people in are country today are trying to get in shape and why, and what the consequences of this fitness obsession are.

The media is probably the biggest factor in creating America's fitness obsession. Television, movies, and especially magazines show people with "perfect" bodies and try to convince us (society as a whole) that these images are what "normal" people should look like. Especially in the case of advertisements, the use of these images of super-thin models are designed to make money. If a company is selling a certain product, like a pair of running shoes for example, they might put a really thin, fit model in their ad to try to make us think that by buying their shoes, we will be thin and have a great body just like the model. Now, many of us would say "Oh, I wouldn't fall for that," but we do, everyday. Gyms, diet-drug manufactures, and companies like Weight Watchers do the same thing: use really thin, "real" people to make us believe we should want to look like this too and that using their products or services will make it happen. Doctors and the medical establishment in general also contribute to the message that "thin is in." It seems like every day a new "study" comes out that links being fat with all kinds of health problems. The message seems to be : lose weight or you could die. With that kind of threat being made, who wouldn't try to lose weight? This too seems to be money-motivated. The more obese people who seek medical help and advice, the more money doctors and hospitals make. It's clear that it's not just companies like Nike and Weight Watchers seeing the benefits of Americans obsession with fitness.

So what's wrong with wanting to be fit? Nothing, really, unless it is taken to extremes. If people want to exercise simply because they want to be healthy, that's fine. When it becomes and obsession, though, it's a bad thing. One of the negative consequences of a fitness obsession is the amount of money wasted on overpriced gyms, diet programs, and diet drugs. Gyms cost a lot of money to join, and most charge monthly dues. Of course, a gym is a business, so it has to charge money, but why pay so much for the same thing you can get by riding your bike, running, or playing a sport, which is free? The same is true for diet drugs and programs. Many of these things cost a lot of money, and many of them don't even work. Thus, people are throwing away a lot of money on useless things that aren't doing them any good, and could even be harming them.

Physical harm is another possible negative consequence. Many diet drugs and diet programs aren't approved by doctors or the FDA, and people have died as a result of using them. Metabolife is a great example. Also, injuries can occur really easily in gyms, especially if a person is working out too hard and too often.

Another really important consequence of this fitness obsession is the psychological impact on the person. Some people get really discouraged when then diet and exercise and don't see instant results. They may get really down on themselves and feel like a failure if they don't get instantly thin and fit. This could lead to depression, which is definitely a negative consequence.

As you can see, there are many factors contributing to the current fitness craze in America, and the results of this craze can be really devastating. From injuries to depression to death, our obsession with fitness is dangerous to us, and it's time we did something to counteract it.

WHAT NEXT? EVALUATING AND REVISING

Many students confuse "revision" with "editing"—they think that preparing an essay for submission to an instructor means looking at and "fixing" sentence errors. BUT you should not yet concentrate on your sentences— unless they are so unclear that YOU do not know what you are trying to say. These are the three major activities of revision.

- Adding content
- Deleting content
- Re-arranging content

These activities should tell you why it may not be a good idea to nit-pick your sentences at this stage. If you spend an hour "perfecting" one sentence and then decide to delete the whole paragraph, you will have wasted an hour.

During the revision process, you should concentrate on the big picture, the essay as a whole. Your answers to the following questions will help you decide what is needed to improve your essay.

DOES THE ESSAY ADDRESS THE ASSIGNMENT DIRECTIONS?

No matter how well written an essay is, if it does not follow the assignment directions, then it will not receive a passing grade. For instance, if your instructor asks you to write on the benefits of joining a health club, but you write your essay on buying exercise equipment, you will not have followed the prompt.

- If you cannot answer "yes" to this question, you will need to go back to the planning stage of the writing process.

Does the Essay Have a Clear Thesis?

Provide a clear thesis for your essay. Trying to read an essay without a thesis can be like driving to a place you've never been before without a road map or directions. At the end of the journey, you know that you have arrived somewhere, but you may or may not know where you are. Because readers can be fickle, you want to make sure your reader knows the "destination." Although your first draft may not have a clear thesis, make sure that your final essay does, make sure it is clearly stated, and for academic writing the best place to put the thesis is towards the beginning of the essay.

- Most writers do not "discover" what it is they are trying to say until the end of the essay, so look carefully at the end of your draft to see if there is a sentence there that reflects the overall focus of your essay. Consider moving this sentence closer to the beginning of the essay.

Does Each Paragraph Have a Clear Topic Sentence?

Again, you should keep your reader clearly informed every step of the journey exactly where he/he is headed—and has been. A clearly stated topic sentence can accomplish this.

- Try to avoid "obvious" and formulaic opening sentences such as
"Another reason why my idea will work is . . ."
OR
"Not only should people join gyms, but they should also . . ."

Note how the two paragraphs below taken from E. B. White's "Education" begin with clear topic sentences that set up the details that follow:

His days were rich in formal experience. Wearing overalls and an old sweater (the accepted uniform of the private seminary), he sallied forth at morn accompanied by a nurse or a parent and walked (or was pulled) two blocks to a corner where the school bus made a flag stop. This flashy vehicle was as punctual as death: seeing us waiting at the cold curb, it would sweep to a half, open its mouth, suck the boy in, and spring away with an angry growl. It was a good deal like a train picking up a bag of mail. At school the scholar was worked on for six or seven hours by half a dozen teachers and a nurse, and was revived on orange juice in mid-morning. In a cinder court he played games supervised by an athletic instructor, and in a cafeteria he ate lunch worked out by a dietician. He soon learned to read with gratifying facility and discernment and to make Indian weapons of a semi-deadly nature. Whenever one of his classmates fell low of a fever the news was put on the wires and there were breathless phone calls to physicians, discussing periods of incubation and allied magic.

In the country all one can say is that the situation is different and somehow more casual. Dressed in corduroys, sweatshirt, and short rubber boots, and carrying a tin dinner-pail, our scholar departs at crack of dawn for the village school, two and a half miles down the road, next to the cemetery. When the road is open and the car will start, he makes the journey by motor, courtesy of his old man. When the snow is deep or the motor is dead or both, he makes it on the hoof. In the afternoons he walks or hitches all or part of the way home in fair weather, gets transported in foul. The schoolhouse is a two-room frame building, bungalow type, shingles stained a burnt brown with weather-resistant stain. It has a chemical toilet in the basement and two teachers above stairs. One takes the first three grades, the other the fourth, fifth, and sixth. They have little or no time for individual instruction, and no time at all for the esoteric. They teach what they know themselves, just as fast and as hard as they can manage. The pupils sit still at their desks in class, and do their milling around outdoors during recess.

Are There Enough Paragraphs to Support the Thesis?

Always think of your thesis as something you MUST prove or defend. reader. If you assume that your reader doesn't share your views and needs to be convinced that your idea is a good one, then you may work harder to support your thesis. Try to read your essay objectively to see if you need to add any more paragraphs to your essay.

Is There Enough Support for the Topic Sentences?

Refer to Chapter 1 for information on developing ideas for your paragraphs.

- Refer to Chapter 1, "The Paragraph," for tips on types of support and methods of organization.
- Note how E. B. White provides lots of details to show the "formal" and "casual" experiences at the different schools.
- Academic paragraphs should be approximately ½ a page long. Very short paragraphs usually need more development. If you have a string of short paragraphs, you may be able to combine them and provide a topic sentence to unify them.

Are the Paragraphs Coherent?

Do the ideas flow logically from one to the next? Although you will know the connections between the ideas, your reader may not, so make sure you have clear language that guides your reader through your paragraph. Refer to the techniques discussed in the "Coherence" section of Chapter 1, and use these tools to improve the flow of your paragraph.

Now You Are Ready to Revise

Armed with the answers to these questions, you should now revise your essay. As you can see, writing is recursive. This means that you do not begin at A and travel in a straight line to Z. For instance, if during the revision stage, you decide that you need to add more details, you will need to do some brainstorming, listing, etc. to come up with those ideas. Refer back to the "Prewriting" section of this chapter for help.

THE FINAL STEP: EDITING AND PROOFREADING

By the time you get to this final step, you will have a lot of time and energy invested in your essay. It would be a shame submit it and receive a lower grade than the paper might otherwise deserve because you have omitted these final steps: editing and proofreading.

Editing

Now is the time to look closely at the sentences.

The most common errors:

Sentence boundary errors
> Run-ons/comma splices
> Fragments

Pronoun errors
> Agreement
> Reference

Unclear sentences
> Missing words
> Extra words
> Words out of order
> Misused words

Part III of this textbook, "The Handbook," will provide help for correcting these errors.

Proofreading

Your essay is now focused, well-developed, coherent, and your sentences correct and varied. You should take the time before turning in the essay to scrutinize it one more time. Be sure to print out a copy at this stage because there are some "bloopers" that you may not be able to pick up on a computer screen. For instance, your printer may omit the last line (or more) of a page, or you may have paragraphs that are two pages long that you can't visually "see" on the computer—this error is not as uncommon as it may seem. You may also have typed words twice, omitted others, or inadvertently pressed a key on the keyboard. Taking the time to look over your essay one last time will mean that you have turned in your best work.

THE FINISHED PRODUCT

Here is the student's revised essay.

America's Obsession with Fitness

Nowadays, it seems that American are obsessed with fitness, especially with achieving the "ideal" body. Millions of Americans go to gyms, take diet pills and other drugs and go on fad diets every day. Why do they do this, and do these things really give people what they are looking for? What are the consequences of America's obsession with fitness? These are complex questions, the answers equally as complex. Granted, some people seek a path of fitness to counter illness or disease. A 35 year-old, for instance, who has just had a heart attack, will probably pay more attention to diet and exercise in order to prolong his/her life. But people in the U.S. today are trying to get in shape for various reasons other than fitness, and the consequences are serious enough that we need to seek some solutions.

One reason that we flock to gyms and diet companies is that we are bombarded by ideal images via the media, probably the biggest factor in creating America's fitness obsession. Television, movies, and especially magazines show people with *perfect* bodies and try to convince us—society as a whole—that these images are what *normal* people should look like. A recent movie, <u>Shallow Hal</u>, depicts a man who has the "gift" of seeing an obese woman as super-thin. He is presumably able to see the "inner" person, but the reactions of his friends who are not blessed by the "gift," constantly remind the audience that if we are obese, we will be shunned and ridiculed—and single. The premise of <u>Shallow Hal</u>, that we should not be obsessed with outer appearances, is a good one. But this message is subsumed by the life this overweight woman leads. Likewise, a recent advertisement for Jenny Craig depicts a thin woman holding a "before" picture. Her shame occurred when a friend mistakenly believed she was pregnant, this reaction propelling her to do something about her appearance. Moreover, a glance at the covers of magazines at the grocery store checkout reinforces the same message. Men and women of ALL ages should take charge of their lives and do everything to achieve the perfect image. The message is clear: If you gain weight you will not look good, you will be ridiculed and shunned, and you had better do something about it.

But are these companies motivated by a genuine concern for the health and well-being of Americans? Probably not. The main concern of most businesses is profit; advertising budgets nationwide run into the billions. Much of this money is spent trying to understand consumers, our fears, our weaknesses, our vulnerabilities. Knowing that we have somehow connected being thin and firm to possessing high morals, gyms, diet-drug manufacturers, and companies like Weight Watchers use really thin people to make us believe we should want to look like this too and that using their products or services will make it happen. Judging by the huge profits these companies make, we readily buy into the sales pitch. However, doctors and the medical establishment in general also contribute to the message that "thin is in." It seems like every day a new "study" comes out that links being fat with all kinds of health problems. The message seems to be: lose weight or you could die. With that kind of threat being made, who wouldn't try to lose weight? This too seems to be money-motivated. The more obese people who seek medical help and advice, the more money doctors and hospitals make. It's clear that it's not just companies like Nike and Weight Watchers seeing the benefits of Americans obsession with fitness.

So what's wrong with wanting to be fit? Nothing, really, unless it is taken to extremes. If people want to exercise simply because they want to be healthy, that's fine. When it becomes an obsession, though, it's a bad thing. One of the negative consequences of a fitness obsession is the amount of money wasted on overpriced gyms, diet programs, and diet drugs. Gyms cost a lot of money to join, and most charge monthly dues. Many also require contracts, so that even if a person stops attending, he/she is still required to pay the monthly dues. Of course, a gym is a business, so it has to charge money, but why pay so much for the same thing you can get by riding your bike, running, or playing a sport, which is free? It also seems strange that people will hire someone to mow their yards and clean their houses while paying for the privilege of exercising at a gym. The same is true for diet drugs and programs. Many of these things cost a lot of money, and many of them don't even work. Thus, people are throwing away a lot of money on useless things that aren't doing them any good, and could even be harming them.

Harm to ourselves is another possible negative consequence—both physical and mental. Many diet drugs and diet programs aren't approved by doctors or the FDA, and people have died as a result of using them. Phen Fen and Metabolife are great examples of "wonder drugs" gone awry. Also, injuries can occur really easily in gyms, especially if a person is working out too hard and too often. We often see the competition that occurs between gym members trying to outdo each other on various machines and in the weight room. And often, we see these people soaking in the Jacuzzi afterwards. Another really important consequence of this fitness obsession is the psychological impact on the person. Some people get really discouraged when they diet and exercise and don't see instant results. They may get really down on themselves and feel like a failure if they don't get instantly thin and fit. This could lead to depression, which is definitely a negative consequence. Sometimes, the obsession also leads to eating disorders, particularly among young women who often seem like they are rejecting their maturing bodies in order to retain an adolescent look forever.

As you can see, there are many factors contributing to the current fitness craze in America, and the results of this craze can be really devastating. From injuries to depression to death, our obsession with fitness is dangerous to us, and it's time we did something to counteract it. What can we do? The most obvious is to accept our bodies for what they are and to recognize that we all can't be the same. It is probably futile, for instance, for most women to strive to achieve a body type that only a very small percentage can. We can also look—really look—at the advertisements we are surrounded with. If we analyze ads closely, we might be able to see the underlying message and how the companies are playing on our fears. We should also acknowledge that the person who eats two or more cookies, the one who can't pass "the pinch test," the one who eats the whole hamburger plus fries, is not a bad person. Health is one thing; obsession is another. We should try to recognize the difference.

CHAPTER 3
Responding to Reading

CRITICAL READING

Reading and writing go hand-in-hand. People who read a lot are usually good writers because reading can

- Increase a writer's vocabulary
- Provide examples of effective sentences
- Enhance critical thinking skills
- Expand knowledge of a variety of issues

REASONS FOR READING

You have probably already discovered in your college classes that your instructors assign a lot of reading. Because reading situations and requirements differ, the way you read the material will differ also. You would not, for instance, read your biology textbook the same way you might read the latest *Harry Potter* book.

Reading for Knowledge/Information

Here are a few instances where you will be extracting information from the reading material:

- History—learning dates, battles, sequences of events
- Biology—examining forms of life, learning terminology
- Newspapers—finding out what has happened in the world
- English
    - Research—finding facts and statistics
    - Handbook—recognizing sentence errors and learning how to fix them

Reading for Models

The essays that you read for English classes can also provide effective—and ineffective—examples of the following:

- Introductions
- Conclusions
- Paragraphs
- Organization
- Types of support
- Techniques of coherence
- Sentences

Reading to Respond

Many essay prompts will ask you to express your opinion about a particular article:

- Do you agree or disagree with the author's views?
- Compare/contrast your views with those of the author.
- Is the author's essay effective? Why or why not?
- Compare/contrast two articles on the same topic.

ACTIVE READING

"Active" reading does not mean that you engage in physical activity while reading: exercising on a Treadmill, climbing on a Stairmaster, running around the block, or doing jumping jacks in the living room. Instead, it is the mind that needs to be active. Have you ever read a paragraph or page from a book six times and still don't know what you have read? Have you read a chapter assigned for homework, but when the instructor begins to ask questions the next day, you cannot recall anything about the chapter? If so, the following tools for active reading may help.

Prepare to Read

Keep in mind as you read that you may not be the target audience; all who write DO NOT necessarily share your views. Therefore you should be careful that you do not "revise" the author's ideas/words so that they project your own opinions. One way to help accomplish this task is to determine the intended audience; try to obtain as much background information as you can BEFORE you begin to read. You should look for information about the following:

- The author
- Publication:
    Where/when was the article published?
    Who usually buys this publication?
- What kind of writing is it? Article? Textbook Chapter?

Ask Questions as You Read

The following questions should help

- What does the title tell you about the article/essay?
- If you had to sum up the author's main point in one sentence, what would you say?
- Does the author use examples to support his or her points? If so, what do the examples illustrate?
- Other than examples, what does the author use to support his or her points?
- Who do you think the author's intended audience is? How do you know?
- Are there any words in the essay/article that are unfamiliar to you? (If so, look them up in the dictionary and note their definitions).
- What is the overall "tone" of the essay/article? Is the tone appropriate to the subject matter and audience? Why or why not?
- What points of the essay/article stand out for you? Why?
- Can you relate anything in the essay/article to your own experiences and/or observations?

Answer the Questions

Of course, as you discover the answers to these questions, you should WRITE them down. You may have been told in high school that you should not write in your books, and this habit may be so ingrained by now that you cannot bring yourself to write in college books. But one of best ways to remember what you have read is to annotate—write directly in the book next to the relevant passage(s). At the very least, try to come up with a "plot summary" as follows:

- Underline the author's thesis—or write it in your own words if the thesis is not directly stated in the essay.
- Briefly summarize each paragraph.
- Explain how each paragraph supports the thesis.

Here are some other tips:

- If you have looked up the meaning of a word in your dictionary, write the definition next to the word.
- Put question marks next to passages that you do not understand OR that you need more information about
- If the author states that there are "several reasons" for something, be sure to number these reasons: 1, 2, 3, etc.
- If you agree with a point, write "yes" next to it; conversely, if you disagree, write "no."

Is he a criminal? (My first victim was a woman—white, well dressed, probably in her late twenties. I came upon her late one evening on a deserted street in Hyde Park, a relatively affluent neighborhood in [*wealthy*] an otherwise mean, impoverished section of Chicago. [*poor*] As I swung onto the avenue behind her, there seemed to be a discreet, uninflammatory [*not causing a strong emotional reaction*] distance between us. Not so. She cast back a worried glance. To her, the youngish black man—a broad six feet two inches with a beard and billowing hair, both hands shoved into the pockets of a bulky military jacket—seemed menacingly close. After a few more quick glimpses, she picked up her pace and was soon running in earnest. [*sincerity*] Within seconds she disappeared into a cross street. [*She fears him because of his race and how he is dressed*]

That was more than a decade ago. I was twenty-two years old, a graduate student newly arrived at the University of Chicago. It was in the echo of that terrified woman's footfalls that I first began to the know the unwieldy [*Difficult to manage*] inheritance I'd come into—the ability to alter public space in ugly ways. It was clear she thought herself the quarry [*prey*] of a mugger, a rapist, or worse. Suffering a bout of insomnia, however, I was stalking sleep, not defenseless wayfarers. As a softy who is scarcely able to take a knife to a raw chicken—let alone hold one to person's throat—I was surprised, embarrassed, and dismayed all at once. (Her flight made me feel like an accomplice in tyranny.) [*He is harmless, and peoples' responses are hurtful.*] It also made it clear that I was indistinguishable from the muggers who occasionally seeped into [*What does he mean?*] the area from the surrounding ghetto. That first encounter, and those that followed, signified that a vast, unnerving gulf lay between nighttime pedestrians—particularly women—and me. And I was soon gathered that being perceived as dangerous is a hazard in itself. I only needed to turn a corner into a dicey [*dangerous or risky*] situation, or crowd some frightened, armed person in a foyer somewhere, or make an errant [*straying*] move after being pulled over by a policeman. Where fear and weapons meet—and they often do in urban America—there is always the possibility of death. [*His life is in danger from the people who are afraid of HIM.*]

THESIS: Because of his race and appearance, people fear and avoid him

Another way to answer the questions is to keep a reading chart for the essays you read.

Choose several points from your assigned reading and fill out the following chart

Point/Quote From the Essay/Article:	My Reaction (What I Think and/or Feel):	Why I Think/Feel This Way:

RESPONDING TO ESSAYS

Writing a Summary

The purpose of summarizing is to take something you have read and re-state it more briefly and in your own words. Since a summary **must** retain the meaning of the original work being summarized, make sure that you understand what you are reading before you begin to write. Here are some guidelines you should follow when writing a summary:

- Begin with the author's thesis and be sure to state the name of the author and the title of the work you are summarizing. Example:

  > In her essay "The 'Fragile American Girl' Myth," Christina Hoff Sommers argues against the notion that American girls and women, like racial minorities and the physically handicapped, are disadvantaged and marginalized members of society and that as such, they are in need of special attention to protect them from victimization.

  > ****Remember:** The first time you refer to the author, use his or her full name. After the first reference, you may refer to the author as "the author" or as "he" or "she" (depending upon the gender of the author) or by his or her LAST name ("Sommers asserts that . . ."). Do not refer to the author only by his or her first name; you do not know him or her personally.

- Put each of the author's supporting points into your own words. Take care to avoid changing the meaning of the author's original points.

- Keep direct quotations to a minimum, but if you do use the author's words, be sure to enclose them in quotation marks.

- It is not necessary to include EVERY example, fact, or statistic the author uses, but you may **briefly** summarize a couple of the most important examples.

- Try to combine the author's ideas into fewer sentences that were used in the original. The idea is to make the summary shorter than the work being summarized; the summary should **never** be longer.

- Use precise, accurate, present-tense verbs when introducing the author's ideas, rather than repeatedly using "says," "talks about," or "writes." Try to choose verbs that accurately reflect the author's purpose. Here is a list of verbs you might choose from:

argues	presents	explains
claims	hints	concludes
asserts	expresses	points out
implies	hypothesizes	declares

infers	speculates	emphasizes
promotes	insinuates	questions
discusses	summarizes	states

Be sure to use a variety of the above verbs.

- Since the summary is NOT a discussion of your opinion, do not use "I."

Avoiding Plagiarism

When incorporating material from other sources into your writing, it is very important to avoid committing **plagiarism.** Plagiarism (from the Greek word for "kidnapper") is using another source's original words, thoughts, ideas, data, etc. without giving credit to the source. All of the following are considered plagiarism:

- Failure to properly cite the source of any material borrowed from an outside source (including books, periodicals, and, of course, the Internet)
- Failure to use quotation marks to distinguish another author's exact words from your own
- Failure to give credit for the paraphrased/summarized ideas of others
- Failure to include bibliographic information for all sources used in your essays
- Submitting any assignment NOT written by you (i.e. an essay written by a friend or purchased from an online essay/term paper "dealer" or an essay copied in its entirety from a book, magazine or other media source)

Whether you do it on purpose or inadvertently, plagiarism is considered a form of cheating, one that can have severe consequences. Though the punishments for plagiarism vary from one school to the next, they can range from failing the plagiarized assignment to being expelled from college. If you are unsure about how to use other sources in your essays, consult your instructor.

A Sample Summary

Read the following summary of "The Fragile American Girl Myth," noting the following:

- Title of the essay, author's name, and author's thesis in the opening sentence
- Active verbs
- Transitions
- Use of author's name and synonyms

- A minimum of direct quotations
- Effective paraphrasing of the author's ideas (see section on paraphrasing below)

In her essay "The Fragile American Girl Myth," Christina Hoff Sommers argues against the notion that American girls and women, like racial minorities and the physically handicapped, are disadvantaged and marginalized members of society, and that as such, they are in need of special attention to protect them from victimization. Sommers offers statistical information to refute the "myth" of the "fragile American girl," citing boys' overall poorer performance in school, their dramatically higher suicide rate, and their more frequent involvement in crime and drug use, among other issues, as examples of the ways in which American males are at a much greater disadvantage than females. She also provides facts, such as women's longer life expectancy and their higher rate of college attendance to further support her argument. While Sommers concedes that some girls do need help and that our society can certainly do more to help them, she insists that there is no credible evidence to suggest that American girls are treated more unfairly and suffer more than boys. Sommers contends that this mistaken idea is perpetuated by feminists who are fixated on proving that society works to oppress women. She claims that research conducted by feminists is flawed and misleading because rather than gathering data and coming to a conclusion about the status of females in America, the researchers come to their conclusions first and then gather information to support these conclusions. Sommers concludes her essay by pointing out that American women have more freedom than women in any other part of the world.

Writing the Evaluative Response

An evaluative response is an essay in which you, the writer, respond to an article or essay written by another author. The evaluative response requires you to briefly **summarize** the author's points, to formulate your own **thesis** in response to the author's points, and to **analyze** the author's argument by providing and supporting your response to the author's main points. Here are some tips for writing the evaluative response essay:

- **Understand what you have read:** Be sure that you understand the thesis and supporting points of the article or essay you are responding to. Read the essay several times, making notes on the author's points and your reactions to them. Find the meanings of any unfamiliar words, first by attempting to understand them in the context of the sentence, and then using your dictionary if you are still unable to figure them out.

- **Formulate your thesis:** Look at what the essay assignment is asking you to do, and formulate a thesis which responds both to the assignment AND to the article or essay you have read. For example, if the assignment asks you to identify the author's thesis and discuss whether or not it is a valid argument, your thesis should include both a statement of the author's thesis AND your opinion as to whether or not the thesis is a valid one.

- **Include a clear introduction:** Your introduction should include the title of the essay or article you are responding to, the author's name, a brief paraphrase of the author's main point(s) and your thesis. Be sure to punctuate and capitalize the title properly (titles of articles and essays should be in quotes) and to spell the author's name correctly as well. Your thesis should be clearly and assertively stated.

- **Provide a BRIEF summary of the author's important points:** Most likely, you will need to briefly summarize some of the author's points in order to respond to them. In summarizing, remember to **put the author's points into your own words, or, if you are using the author's exact words, put them in quotes.** Refer to the author by **last name only** (except in your introduction when you will use both the first AND last name), and use **present tense verbs** in presenting the author's points (i.e. "Mills *claims*. . ." or "Sommers *argues*. . .") ****Remember: The idea is to briefly summarize some of the <u>key</u> points of the essay for the purpose of responding to them. DON'T summarize the entire essay without responding to it!**

- **Provide your own analysis of the author's points:** Be sure to support your analysis with **specific** facts, examples, etc., and clearly connect these examples to YOUR thesis and the author's points. Do not leave it up to the reader to figure out how your examples connect to the topic and to your thesis.

- **Include a conclusion:** Your conclusion should briefly "sum up" your response to the article or essay. It is certainly acceptable to re-state (briefly) the points you've made in your essay.

The Introduction

If you are asked to write an evaluative response essay that is, for instance, 2 1/2 pages long, it makes no sense to spend a page and a half "clearing your throat" before getting to the point you wish to make. Each of the following introduce an essay written in response to Brent Staples' "Black Men and Public Space." Read these introductions carefully and see if you detect any problems—refer back to Chapter 1, The Thesis and The Introduction.

- Since the beginning of time, throughout all the ages, we as human beings have been involved with relationships with other humans. Sometimes we have problems in these relationships. Other times we get along just fine. Some of these problems include problems with: love, family, financial things, children, work, cars, and all the other things that we human beings have to deal with every day of our lives, day in and day out. One such person that knows about these problems is Brent Staples who wrote an essay called "Black Men and Public Space." Brent talks about a black man dressed in weird clothes who wanders around the streets of a big city late at night and he scares people. This is a good essay and I liked it. In my essay I'm going to tell you why I agree with Brent Staples' thesis.

- In this essay, I will explain what Brent Staples' thesis is and whether or not I agree with him.

- What is racism? What is stereotyping? Why do these things happen? Will we ever overcome them? Brent Staples tries to answer these heavy-duty questions in his essay "Black Men and Public Space." And he does a good job too. So yes, I agree with Brent.

- You just never know when someone's going to be afraid of you. Brent Staples in his essay "Black Men and Public Space" talks about a time when someone was scared of him. I had an experience last year when I was afraid. I was in the mall parking lot and it was late at night and I saw a gang of boys by my car talking. I didn't know what to do, just like Brent. So I whipped out my cell phone and called my dad and told him I was scared. And my dad said, "Just wait there; I'll be there in a minute." And he came in his big Ford Ranger and he just pulled right up behind my car and got out and those boys just left. And so I walked over to my car, kissed my dad, and went on home. So I know what fear is and I can relate to Brent's experiences about fear because just like him I was in a public space like the mall.

It is evident that the above introductions are not effective beginnings for an evaluative response. So how should you begin this type of essay? You may use any of the techniques for effective introductions included in Chapter 1, but there are four items that MUST be in your introduction.

- The title of the essay
- The author's full name
- The author's thesis
     May also contain a brief summary of the main points
- Your thesis

If you include the above, you are letting your reader know that

- your essay is indeed responding to another essay,
- you fully understand what the author is saying, and
- you have devised a thesis of your own in response to the reading.

Examine the following effective introduction to an essay responding to "Black Men and Public Space."

In "Black Men and Public Space," Brent Staples argues that he—and other African American men—have the ability to "alter public space in ugly ways." He describes incidents from his life when others, "black, white, male, or female" physically moved away from him. Through these encounters, Staples claims, he learned "the language of fear." In fact, the author's carefully selected language—particularly those words that conjure up images of war—

help the reader understand and empathize. However, African American men are not the only ones who can "alter public space." The same can be said of people from other ethnic backgrounds, women, and/or anyone who appears "different" in any way.

Incorporating Sources

An evaluative response essay does more then merely summarize the source essay and provide your own view on the topic addressed in the essay. Your job is to include and **analyze** evidence from the source essay.

Paraphrasing

One way to include the author's ideas in your own essay is to paraphrase. Paraphrase, like summary, requires that you put the author's ideas in your own words; however, unlike the summary, the paraphrase is not always shorter than the original. First, read the following passage from "The Fragile American Girl Myth."

> This is not to deny that some girls are in serious trouble, or that we can't do better by girls, educationally and otherwise. What I am saying is, you can't find any responsible research that shows that girls, as a group, are worse off than boys, or that girls are an underprivileged class.

Now, let us look at two paraphrases of this passage.

> Paraphrase #1:
> Sommers can't deny that many girls are in trouble. She also claims that we should do more to educate girls. But she says that there is no credible research to show that girls are not as well off as boys or that girls are of a lesser class.

> Paraphrase #2:
> While Sommers concedes that some girls do need help and that our society can certainly do more to help them, she insists that there is no credible evidence to suggest that American girls are treated more unfairly and suffer more than boys.

Note how in Paraphrase #1, the writer uses phrases that almost mirror the original. For instance, "not to deny that some girls are in serious trouble" becomes "can't deny that many girls are in trouble." And "responsible research that shows that girls . . . are worse off than boys" becomes "credible research to show that girls are not as well off as boys."

Paraphrase #2, though, keeps the original ideas but expresses them in the writer's own words and is therefore the more effective paraphrase.

Quotations

There will, of course, be instances when it is not possible—or desirable—to use only paraphrases. The source essay may contain phrases that need to be quoted. Here are a few tips for effectively including quotations in your writing.

- Avoid "orphan" quotes.

Brent Staples talks about his walks at night. "She cast back a worried glance." He further states that things did not improve over the years.

Note how there is nothing to connect this quote to either the sentence before and/or the sentence after it. The reader has to work hard to see the connections.

- Don't just "string" quotes together.

Staples claims that his "first victim was a woman" and he "came upon her late one evening on a deserted street in Hyde Park" and that "there seemed to be a discreet uninflammatory distance between us," but that she "cast back a worried glance" because he seemed to be "menancingly close."

Use the quotes to support and enhance your ideas, not to "do the talking for you."

- Make sure the quotation makes sense in your sentence, that it is clear and grammatically correct. If you change any words in the original, use [brackets]. For instance, if the quote begins with a pronoun that references a noun in the original, you may need to change the pronoun to a noun.

I often witness that "hunch posture," from women after dark on the warren-like streets of Brooklyn where I live. They seem to set their faces on neutral, . . .

In this passage, the "they" refers to "women." If you want to use the clause "they seem to set their faces on neutral," you will need to clarify the pronoun reference.

Staples explains how "[the women] set their faces on neutral," in order to . . .

Similarly, you may need to change the verb tense of the original

Staples explains how he had "often [witnessed] that 'hunch posture' from women after dark."

One good way to make sure your quotes are effectively incorporated into your work is to think of a sandwich. Just as the top and bottom slices

of bread hold the sandwich filling in place, a writer's lead in and analysis will hold the quoted material together.

- **The lead in,** or top slice of bread, should identify the author and provide some context for the quote to follow.
- **The quotation,** or filling, follows.
- **The analysis or discussion** of the quotation will clarify the author's words if necessary and show how the ideas support your own thesis.

The following successful "sandwiches" all use parts of the following passage from Brent Staples' essay.

> I often witness that "hunch posture," from women after dark on the warrenlike streets of Brooklyn where I live. They seem to set their faces on neutral and, with their purse straps strung across their chests bandolier style, they forge ahead as though bracing themselves against being tackled.

Sandwich #1:
African American men are often stereotyped as being dangerous. This can be seen in the accounts of writer Brent Staples' essay "Black Men and Public Space." He vividly explains, "They seem to set their faces on neutral and, with their purse straps strung bandolier style across their chests, they forge ahead as though bracing themselves against being tackled." His experiences show that in today's society in a time of alleged equality, people are still treated differently because of their color.

Sandwich #2:
Despite efforts to eliminate harmful stereotypes in society, some people's deep down fears—fears that are a result of stereotypes—remain. As author Brent Staples, in his essay "Black Men and Public Space" gives the example, "they seem to set their faces on neutral and, with their purse straps strung bandolier style across their chests, they forge ahead as though bracing themselves against being tackled." Such a reaction is not uncommon.

Sandwich #3
In "Black Men and Public Space," Brent Staples describes the posture of women who walk at night: "They seem to set their faces on neutral and, with their purse straps strung across their chests bandolier style, they forge ahead as though bracing themselves against being tackled." Staples suggests that these women need to play multiple roles. They must appear to be indifferent to their environment and not make eye contact as they "set their faces on neutral." Further they become soldiers with bandoliers and defensive football players guarding themselves against being attacked.

WRITING THE IN-CLASS ESSAY

In many college classes, in both English and other subjects, you will be required to write timed essays in class. Often, these in-class essays will be midterms or final exams that will constitute a significant portion of your final grade in the class. Because of the time constraints, and because of the weight many instructors place on in-class essays in calculating final course grades, these writing assignments can be a source of worry, even dread, for college writers, and this worry and dread can cause a writer to "freeze up" or experience "writer's block" during a timed essay test. Writing the in-class essay, however, need not be as scary as jumping out of an airplane or riding the biggest, fastest rollercoaster in the world. The anxiety and fear stemming from in-class writing **can** be overcome; all it takes is some preparation, determination, and effective time management. The following are some helpful hints for writing a timed essay in class:

- ✏ **Understand what you are being asked to do.** Many students make the mistake of reading an essay exam prompt or question once and then quickly jumping directly into writing the essay. Read the prompt/question to yourself several times, noting key words and phrases such as "argue," "explain," "discuss," "compare and contrast," "agree or disagree," etc. These key words and phrases will help you to focus your essay on a particular task – i.e. agreeing or disagreeing with the author of an article you have read for the exam. In many cases, you will have a good idea of what you will be writing about before you even get to class (i.e. if you will be responding to something you have read for homework), so you can begin at home to consider possible questions/prompts you might be given.

- ✏ **Do some pre-writing and planning before you begin writing.** Once you know what you are being asked to do, you can move on to brainstorming and pre-writing. As discussed in Chapter 2, pre-writing is the first step in the writing process; it is an effective way of getting your ideas on paper so that you can see what you think about a particular topic. Choose one of the pre-writing strategies discussed in Chapter 2—the one that you feel works best for you—and formulate some thoughts on a piece of scratch paper before you start writing your actual essay. For example, if you agree with the author of the article you are responding to, you might use "listing" to come up with a list of reasons **why** you agree with the author. Once you have done your pre-writing, you can formulate your thesis and work on coming up with your supporting points.

- ✏ **Decide on a thesis before you begin writing.** As discussed in Chapter 1, the thesis is perhaps the most important part of the essay, as it provides a focus for the essay and keeps it from wandering off-topic. Before you even begin writing your introduction, you should write your thesis on a piece of scratch paper so that you can have it in front of you as you come up with your supporting points. Refer to Chapter 1 for tips on writing good thesis statements.

✏ **Jot down some supporting points.** Using your thesis and pre-writing as guides, decide on the points you will use to support your thesis. Remember, a good college essay provides several relevant, well-developed supporting points. Try to avoid falling into the five-paragraph essay "formula" in which writers limit themselves to an introduction, conclusion, and three body paragraphs. If you have **two** strong supporting points that you can fully develop, make them! Likewise, if you have **six** strong points to make, **do not** limit yourself to only three. You will, of course, need to take into consideration the time limit on the in-class essay when deciding on how many supporting points to include.

✏ **Use effective time-management strategies.** Time is a crucial element when writing a timed in-class essay, and it is the element that causes the most needless stress and anxiety for students. Before you begin writing (perhaps even at home, before you get to school), consider the amount of time you have to write the essay, and make a "strategy" for writing, revising, and editing your essay in the allotted time. A time-management strategy for a 2-hour test period might look something like this:

Reading and understanding the prompt	5 minutes
Brainstorming/pre-writing	10 minutes
Composing thesis/jotting down supporting points	5 minutes
Writing the essay	70 minutes
Revising and editing (including re-copying, if needed)	30 minutes**
TOTAL	120 minutes

Note: Depending on the amount of time you are allotted to write, you should consider writing a rough draft AND a final draft. If it appears that you will not have time to do two drafts, try to write your rough draft as neatly as possible, skipping every other line on the paper to allow for minor revisions and corrections.

Dos and Don'ts of Writing In-class Essays

Do. . .

- **Prepare as much as possible in advance of the test date.** This preparation should include reviewing the material you will be writing about (if provided in advance) and considering possible questions or prompts you will be asked to respond to. If your teacher allows notes to be brought into the test, write your notes clearly and concisely several days before the exam to give yourself time to review them. Along this same line, come to the test prepared with the necessary materials (extra pens, pencils, paper, etc.)

- **Bring supplemental materials (if permitted) to the test.** If your teacher allows reference materials such as notes (see above), dictionaries, or grammar review books/sheets, bring them. Though you may not end up using them, if you are permitted to, they could be very helpful to you.

- **Get a good night's sleep and have a good breakfast before the test.** Studies have proven that adequate sleep and good nutrition enhance academic performance. If you are tired, hungry, or just plain run-down, you might not be able to concentrate, and this could interfere with your ability to write a good essay.

- **Use as much of the testing time as you need.** A good rule of thumb is if you are given two hours, USE the two hours. Though you may finish writing before the time is up, you should use as much of the remaining time as possible to read over your essay and make necessary revisions and corrections.

Don't . . .

- **Panic.** One of the major contributing factors to students' failure of timed in-class essays is panic, which in turn leads to "writer's block." If you start to feel nervous, take some deep breaths and remind yourself that you have been given the tools to write an effective in-class essay; all you have to do is use those tools. Focus on your thesis and on the time-management strategy you have formulated.

- **Sit for long periods of time without writing.** When writing a timed essay, you will occasionally hit a point where you will not be able to think of what to say next. When this happens, stopping to "think" might *seem* like a good idea; however, it is likely that the longer you pause, the further you may get from what you were saying before you put down your pen, and you could end up losing your train of thought entirely. If you come to a point where you are not sure what to say, pause **briefly** to read over what you have written so far, and, if necessary, do a bit of freewriting on a separate sheet of scratch paper. The idea is to keep your pen active for as much of the allotted time as possible.

- **Use up a significant portion of your writing time correcting errors.** Remember that writing is a **process,** and that editing is generally the LAST step in that process. If you get too bogged down with spelling, punctuation, capitalization, etc., as you are writing, you might end up using too much of the time you could have spent actually writing and developing your essay, and you could run out of time without finishing your essay. Save editing and correction of errors until the very end, after you have had adequate time to complete your essay. ****Note:** Refer to the time management strategies suggested previously.

PART II
THE READER

THEMATIC CONTENTS

CHAPTER 4

Narration and Description

NARRATION AND DESCRIPTION: USING PERSONAL EXPERIENCES TO MAKE A POINT

In college, you may be asked to write a narrative and/or descriptive essay, but it is more likely that you will be called upon to use these skills to provide support in an essay that uses other devices as well. For instance, if you are arguing that we need to do more to stop child abuse in families, you may narrate—i.e. tell the story—of one child's life and/or you may describe the abuse this child receives. Therefore, these are important skills for any writer to develop.

Narration

Writing narrative comes naturally to most people, and it should because we are constantly being asked to "tell" a story about something. Examine the following.

- At a job interview, you are asked about your previous job experience.
- Your sister asks you what you've been doing for the past month.
- A friend asks you what you did on your vacation.

Responses to all of these questions will usually be given in chronological order, i.e. "I did this, and then I did this, etc."

Although narrative is fairly "easy" to write, many instructors are often disappointed with their students' narrative essays. To explain why, let's consider the qualities that make narration good. It should

- **Have a purpose:** Without a reason to read your narrative, a reader will not be interested. Therefore, instead of just "telling your story," have a purpose. For instance, if you have been the victim of crime, your purpose may be to warn your readers about the consequences of walking alone through a city park late at night. Or if your narrative is about the day you were fired from a job, your purpose may be to let readers know what they shouldn't do in the workplace OR how unfair some employers can be.

- **Have focus:** If you are going to write about an incident when you were mugged, and your purpose is to show readers how dangerous the downtown area can be late at night, you should include only those details that are relevant to this purpose. For instance, if the incident occurred AFTER dinner, you probably don't need to include details about the meal, or—heaven forbid—go back to moment of birth: I was born on the fourth of July . . . Provide just enough background information to place yourself at the scene. Notice in "Workers" how much about the author we learn from his short introduction. We know, for instance, that he comes from a poor family even though he doesn't describe in great detail what his family life was like.

- **Be logically organized:** Usually narratives are written in chronological order, but you may want to begin with the "end" of the incident and then go back to describe how you ended up this way. Be sure to include suitable transitions in your writing so that the reader can follow your narrative. See Chapter 1 for a list of transitions, particularly those "to indicate time and sequence."

- **Show, not tell:** This is probably the greatest "error" many students make in writing narrative. And for this reason, writing good description is a part of being able to write good narrative. You may be able to tell that you are "telling" rather than "showing" if a lot of your sentences begin with the word "I."

Description

When you write description, your "role" is to paint a picture with words for your reader. As in the writing of good narration, provide enough details to convey your ideas and to support your main point. For instance, if you are describing an accident that changed your life, and you want to show how looking at your injured friend made you realize that you should change our driving habits, your description should probably focus on **your friend and her injuries,** not the boy on the bicycle two blocks away. Good description should

- **Be logically organized:** When you describe something, you need to use spatial organization, i.e. where something is in relation to something else. For instance, if you are describing your room and begin at the door, then jump across to the window, over to the closet on the left, back to the window, then to the plant just inside the doorway, your reader will be confused: she or he will not be able to follow you. Your description should be so well organized that if ten people were to draw what you are describing, their pictures should all look nearly alike—allowing of course for differing levels of artistic ability. Other organization strategies to consider are

- Top to bottom—or the reverse
- Inside to outside—or the reverse
- Largest to smallest item, etc.

- **Be vivid and specific:** For instance, the sentence "My father is a big man" doesn't offer the reader much to help picture your father. A person who is four feet six inches tall and weighs eighty pounds will have a different opinion of what constitutes a "big" person than someone who is perhaps 6 ft tall and weighs two hundred pounds. Notice how the following statements become more vivid and specific.
  - My father is a big man.
  - My father is six feet tall and weighs over two hundred pounds.
  - When my father enters our house, his hair brushes the top of the opening and his shoulders barely fit through the doorway.

- **Use sensory images:** Using descriptive details that rely on the senses—sight, touch, hearing, taste, smell—will help draw your reader into your description. For instance, in describing an accident, you could use the following:
  - The windshield shattered on impact. (sight and hearing)
  - The gas tank ruptured, allowing gasoline to spill all over the roadway. (sight and smell)
  - When the other driver spoke to me, I could tell he had been drinking. (smell)
  - A jagged piece of glass pierced my upper arm. (sight and touch)
  - My lip was cut, and my mouth was filled with blood. (sight, taste, touch)

Workers

Richard Rodriguez

It was at Stanford, one day near the end of my senior year, that a friend told me about a summer construction job he knew was available. I was quickly alert. Desire uncoiled within me. My friend said that he knew I had been looking for summer employment. He knew I needed some money. Almost apologetically he explained: It was something I probably wouldn't be interested in, but a friend of his, a contractor, needed someone for the summer to do menial jobs. There would be lots of shoveling and raking and sweeping. Nothing too hard. But nothing more interesting either. Still, the pay would be good. Did I want it? Or did I know someone who did?

I did. Yes, I said, surprised to hear myself say it.

In the weeks following, friends cautioned that I had no idea how hard physical labor really is. ("You only *think* you know what it is like to shovel for eight hours straight.") Their objections seemed to me challenges. They resolved the issue. I became happy with my plan. I decided, however, not to tell my parents. I wouldn't tell my mother because I could guess her worried reaction. I would tell my father only after the summer was over, when I could announce that, after all, I did know what "real work" is like.

The day I met the contractor (a Princeton graduate, it turned out), he asked me whether I had done any physical labor before. "In high school, during the summer," I lied. And although he seemed to regard me with skepticism, he decided to give me a try. Several days later, expectant, I arrived at my first construction site. I would take off my shirt to the sun. And at last grasp desired sensation. No longer afraid. At last become like a *bracero*. "We need those tree stumps out of here by tomorrow," the contractor said. I started to work.

I labored with excitement that first morning—and all the days after. The work was harder than I could have expected. But it was never as tedious as my friends had warned me it would be. There was too much physical pleasure in the labor. Especially early in the day, I would be most alert to the sensations of movement and straining. Beginning around seven each morning (when the air was still damp but the scent of weeds and dry earth anticipated the heat of the sun), I would feel my body resist the first thrusts of the shovel. My arms, tightened by sleep, would gradually loosen; after only several minutes, sweat would gather in beads on my forehead and then—a short while later—I would feel my chest silky with sweat in the breeze. I would return to my work: A nervous spark of pain would fly up my arm and settle to burn like an ember in the thick of my shoulder. An hour, two passed. Three. My whole body would assume regular movements; my shoveling would be described by identical, even movements. Even later in the day, my enthusiasm for primitive sensation would survive the heat and the dust and the insects pricking my back. I would strain wildly for sensation as the day came to a close. At three-thirty, quitting time, I would stand upright and slowly let my head fall back, luxuriating in the feeling of tightness relieved.

Some of the men working nearby would watch me and laugh. Two or three of the older men took the trouble to teach me the right way to use a pick, the correct way to shovel. "You're doing it wrong, too fucking hard," one man scolded. Then proceeded to show me—what persons who work with their bodies all their lives quickly learn—the most economical way to use one's body in labor.

"Don't make your back do so much work," he instructed. I stood impatiently listening, half listening, vaguely watching, then noticed his work-thickened fingers clutching the shovel. I was annoyed. I wanted to tell him that I enjoyed shoveling the wrong way. And I didn't want to learn the right way. I wasn't afraid of back pain. I liked the way my body felt sore at the end of the day.

I was about to, but, as it turned out, I didn't say a thing. Rather it was at that moment I realized that I was fooling myself if I expected a few weeks of labor to gain me admission to the world of the laborer. I would not learn in three months what my father had meant by "real work." I was not bound to this job; I could imagine its rapid conclusion. For me the sensations were to be feared. Fatigue took a different toll on their bodies—and minds.

It was, I know, a simple insight. But it was with this realization that I took my first step that summer toward realizing something even more important about the "worker." In the company of carpenters, electricians, plumbers, and painters at lunch, I would often sit quietly, observant. I was not shy in such company. I felt easy, pleased by the knowledge that I was casually accepted, my presence taken for granted by men (exotics) who worked with their hands. Some days the younger men would talk and talk about sex, and they would howl at women who drove by in cars. Other days the talk at lunchtime was subdued; men gathered in separate groups. It depended on who was around. There were rough, good-natured workers. Others were quiet. The more I remember that summer, the more I realize that there was no single *type* of worker. I am embarrassed to say I had not expected such diversity. I certainly had not expected to meet, for example, a plumber who was an abstract painter in his off hours and admired the work of Mark Rothko. Nor did I expect to meet so many workers with college diplomas. (They were the ones who were not surprised that I intended to enter graduate school in the fall.) I suppose what I really want to say here is painfully obvious, but I must say it nevertheless: The men of that summer were middle-class Americans. They certainly didn't constitute an oppressed society. Carefully completing their work sheets; talking about the fortunes of local football teams; planning Las Vegas vacations; comparing the gas mileage of various makes of campers—they were not *los pobres* my mother had spoken about.

On two occasions, the contractor hired a group of Mexican aliens. They were employed to cut down some trees and haul off debris. In all, there were six men of varying age. The youngest in his late twenties; the oldest (his father?) perhaps sixty years old. They came and they left in a single old truck. Anonymous men. They were never introduced to the other men at the site. Immediately upon their arrival, they would follow the contractor's directions, start working—rarely resting—seemingly driven by a fatalistic sense that work which had to be done was best done as quickly as possible.

I watched them sometimes. Perhaps they watched me. The only time I saw them pay me much notice was one day at lunchtime when I was laughing with the other men. The Mexicans sat apart when they ate, just as they worked by themselves. Quiet. I rarely heard them say much to each other. All I could hear were their voices calling out sharply to one another, giving directions. Otherwise, when they stood briefly resting, they talked among themselves in voices too hard to overhear.

The contractor knew enough Spanish, and the Mexicans—or at least the oldest of them, their spokesman—seemed to know enough English to communicate. But because I was around, the contractor decided one day to make me his translator. (He assumed I could speak Spanish.) I did what I was told. Shyly I went over to tell the Mexicans that the *patrón* wanted them to do something else before they left for the day. As I started to speak, I was afraid with my old fear that I would be unable to pronounce the Spanish words. But it was a simple instruction I had to convey. I could say it in phrases.

The dark sweating faces turned toward me as I spoke. They stopped their work to hear me. Each nodded in response. I stood there. I wanted to say something more. But what could I say in Spanish, even if I could have pronounced the words right? Perhaps I just wanted to engage them in small talk, to be assured of their confidence, our familiarity. I thought for a moment to ask them where in Mexico they were from. Something like that. And maybe I wanted to tell them (a lie, if need be) that my parents were from the same part of Mexico.

I stood there.

Their faces watched me. The eyes of the man directly in front of me moved slowly over my shoulder, and I turned to follow his glance toward *el patrón* some distance away. For a moment I felt swept up by that glance into the Mexicans' company. But then I heard one of them returning to work. And then the others went back to work. I left them without saying anything more.

When they had finished, the contractor went over to pay them in cash. (He later told me that he paid them collectively—"for the job," though he wouldn't tell me their wages. He said something quickly about the good rate of exchange "in their own country.") I can still hear the loudly confident voice he used with the Mexicans. It was the sound of the *gringo* I had heard as a very young boy. And I can still hear the quiet, indistinct sounds of the Mexican, the oldest, who replied. At hearing that voice I was sad for the Mexicans. Depressed by their vulnerability. Angry at myself. The adventure of the summer seemed suddenly ludicrous. I would not shorten the distance I felt from *los pobres* with a few weeks of physical labor. I would not become like them. They were different from me.

After that summer, a great deal—and not very much really—changed in my life. The curse of physical shame was broken by the sun; I was no longer ashamed of my body. No longer would I deny myself the pleasing sensations of my maleness. During those years when middle-class black Americans began to assert with pride, "Black is beautiful," I was able to regard my complexion without shame. I am today darker than I ever was as a boy. I have taken up the middle-class sport of long-distance running. Nearly every day now I run ten or fifteen miles, barely clothed, my skin exposed to the California winter rain and wind or the summer sun of late afternoon. The torso, the soccer player's calves and thighs, the arms of the twenty-year-old I never was, I possess now in my thirties. I study the youthful parody shape in the mirror: the stomach lipped tight by muscle; the shoulders rounded by chin-ups; the arms veined strong. This man. A man. I meet him. He laughs to see me, what I have become.

The dandy. I wear double-breasted Italian suits and custom-made English shoes. I resemble no one so much as my father—the man pictured in those honeymoon photos. At that point in life when he abandoned the dandy's posture, I assume it. At the point when my parents would not consider going on vacation, I register at the Hotel Carlyle in New York and the Plaza Athenée in Paris. I am as taken by the symbols of leisure and wealth as they were. For my parents, however, those symbols became taunts, reminders of all they could not achieve in one lifetime. For me those same symbols are reassuring reminders of public success. I tempt vulgarity to be reassured. I am filled with the gaudy delight, the monstrous grace of the nouveau riche.

In recent years I have had occasion to lecture in ghetto high schools. There I see students of remarkable style and physical grace. (One can see more dandies in such schools than one ever will find in middle-class high schools.) There is not the look of casual assurance I saw students at Stanford display. Ghetto girls mimic high-fashion models. Their dresses are of bold, forceful color; their figures elegant, long; the stance theatrical. Boys wear shirts that grip at their overdeveloped muscular bodies. (Against a powerless future, they engage images of strength.) Bad nutrition does not yet tell. Great disappointment, fatal to youth, awaits them still. For the moment, movements in school hallways are dancelike, a procession of postures in a sexual masque. Watching them, I feel a kind of envy. I wonder how different my adolescence would have been had I been free. . . . But no, it is my parents I see—their optimism during those years when they were entertained by Italian grand opera.

The registration clerk in London wonders if I have just been to Switzerland. And the man who carries my luggage in New York guesses the Caribbean. My complexion becomes a mark of my leisure. Yet no one would regard my complexion the same way if I entered such hotels through the service entrance. That is only to say that my complexion assumes its significance from the context of my life. My skin, in itself, means nothing. I stress the point because I know there are people who would label me "disadvantaged" because of my color. They make the same mistake I made as a boy, when I thought a disadvantaged life was circumscribed by particular occupations. That summer I worked in the sun may have made me physically indistinguishable from the Mexicans working nearby. (My skin was actually darker because, unlike them, I worked without wearing a shirt. By late August my hands were probably as tough as theirs.) But I was not one of *los pobres*. What made me different from them was an attitude of *mind*, my imagination of myself.

I do not blame my mother for warning me away from the sun when I was young. In a world where her brother had become an old man in his twenties because he was dark, my complexion was something to worry about. "Don't run in the sun," she warns me today. I run. In the end, my father was right—though perhaps he did not know how right or why—to say that I would never know what real work is. I will never know what he felt at his last factory job. If tomorrow I worked at some kind of factory, it would go differently for me. My long education would favor me. I could act as a public person—able to defend my interests, to unionize, to petition, to speak up—to challenge and demand. (I will never know what real work is.) I will never know what the Mexicans knew, gathering their shovels and ladders and saws.

Their silence stays with me now. The wages those Mexicans received for their labor were only a measure of their disadvantaged condition. Their silence is more telling. They lack a public identity. They remain profoundly alien. Persons apart. People lacking a union obviously, people without grounds. They depend upon the relative good will or fairness of their employers each day. For such people, lacking a better alternative, it is not such an unreasonable risk.

Their silence stays with me. I have taken these many words to describe its impact. Only: the quiet. Something uncanny about it. Its compliance. Vulnerability. Pathos. As I heard their truck rumbling away, I shuddered, my face mirrored with sweat. I had finally come face to face with *los pobres*.

QUESTIONS FOR DISCUSSION

1. What do we learn about Rodriguez from the first paragraph?
2. Other than for money, what spurred Rodriguez to accept the job?
3. Exactly what did Rodriguez learn from his summer job?

QUESTIONS FOR WRITING

1. Compare/contrast Rodriguez before and after his experience.
2. Using the techniques for writing good narrative and description discussed in this chapter, write about an event in your own life that changed you in some way.

Eleven

Sandra Cisneros

What they don't understand about birthdays and what they never tell you is that when you're eleven, you're also ten, and nine, and eight, and seven, and six, and five, and four, and three, and two, and one. And when you wake up on your eleventh birthday you expect to feel eleven, but you don't. You open your eyes and everything's just like yesterday, only it's today. And you don't feel eleven at all. You feel like you're still ten. And you are—underneath the year that makes you eleven.

Like some days you might say something stupid, and that's the part of you that's still ten. Or maybe some days you might need to sit on your mama's lap because you're scared, and that's the part of you that's five. And maybe one day when you're all grown up maybe you will need to cry like if you're three, and that's okay. That's what I tell Mama when she's sad and needs to cry. Maybe she's feeling three.

Because the way you grow old is kind of like an onion or like the rings inside a tree trunk or like my little wooden dolls that fit one inside the other, each year inside the next one. That's how being eleven years old is.

You don't feel eleven. Not right away. It takes a few days, weeks even, sometimes even months before you say Eleven when they ask you. And you don't feel smart eleven, not until you're almost twelve. That's the way it is.

Only today I wish I didn't have only eleven years rattling inside me like pennies in a tin Band-Aid box. Today I wish I was one hundred and two instead of eleven because if I was one hundred and two I'd have known what to say when Mrs. Price put the red sweater on my desk. I would've known how to tell her it wasn't mine instead of just sitting there with that look on my face and nothing coming out of my mouth.

"Whose is this?" Mrs. Price says, and she holds the red sweater up in the air for all the class to see. "Whose? It's been sitting in the coatroom for a month."

"Not mine," says everybody. "Not me."

"It has to belong to somebody," Mrs. Price keeps saying, but nobody can remember. It's an ugly sweater with red plastic buttons and a collar and sleeves all stretched out like you could use it for a jump rope. It's maybe a thousand years old and even if it belonged to me I wouldn't say so.

Maybe because I'm skinny, maybe because she doesn't like me, that stupid Sylvia Saldívar says, "I think it belongs to Rachel." An ugly sweater like that, all raggedy and old, but Mrs. Price believes her. Mrs. Price takes the sweater and puts it right on my desk, but when I open my mouth nothing comes out.

"That's not, I don't, you're not . . . Not mine," I finally say in a little voice that was maybe me when I was four.

"Of course it's yours," Mrs. Price says. "I remember you wearing it once." Because she's older and the teacher, she's right and I'm not.

Not mine, not mine, not mine, but Mrs. Price is already turning to page thirty-two, and math problem number four. I don't know why but all of a sudden I'm feeling sick inside, like the part of me that's three wants to come out of my eyes, only I squeeze them shut tight and bite down on my teeth real hard and try to remember today I am eleven, eleven. Mama is making a cake for me for tonight, and when Papa comes home everybody will sing Happy birthday, happy birthday to you.

But when the sick feeling goes away and I open my eyes, the red sweater's still sitting there like a big red mountain. I move the red sweater to the corner of my desk with my ruler. I move my pencil and books and eraser as far from it as possible. I even move my chair a little to the right. Not mine, not mine, not mine.

In my head I'm thinking how long till lunchtime, how long till I can take the red sweater and throw it over the schoolyard fence, or leave it hanging on a parking meter, or bunch it up into a little ball and toss it in the alley. Except when math period ends Mrs. Price says loud and in front of everybody, "Now, Rachel, that's enough," because she sees I've shoved the red sweater to the tippy-tip corner of my desk and it's hanging all over the edge like a waterfall, but I don't care.

"Rachel," Mrs. Price says. She says it like she's getting mad. "You put that sweater on right now and no more nonsense."

"But it's not—"

"Now!" Mrs. Price says.

This is when I wish I wasn't eleven, because all the years inside of me—ten, nine, eight, seven, six, five, four, three, two, and one—are pushing at the back of my eyes when I put one arm through one sleeve of the sweater that smells like cottage cheese, and then the other arm through the other and stand there with my arms apart like if the sweater hurts me and it does, all itchy and full of germs that aren't even mine.

That's when everything I've been holding in since this morning, since when Mrs. Price put the sweater on my desk, finally lets go, and all of a sudden I'm crying in front of everybody. I wish I was invisible but I'm not. I'm eleven and it's my birthday today and I'm crying like I'm three in front of everybody. I put my head down on the desk and bury my face in my stupid clown-sweater arms. My face all hot and spit coming out of my mouth because I can't stop the little animal noises from coming out of me, until there aren't any more tears left in my eyes, and it's just my body shaking like when you have the hiccups, and my whole head hurts like when you drink milk too fast.

But the worst part is right before the bell rings for lunch. That stupid Phyllis Lopez, who is even dumber than Sylvia Saldívar, says she remembers the red sweater is hers! I take it off right away and give it to her, only Mrs. Price pretends like everything's okay.

Today I'm eleven. There's a cake Mama's making for tonight, and when Papa comes home from work we'll eat it. There'll be candles and presents and everybody will sing Happy birthday, happy birthday to you, Rachel, only it's too late.

I'm eleven today. I'm eleven, ten, nine, eight, seven, six, five, four, three, two, and one, but I wish I was one hundred and two. I wish I was anything but eleven, because I want today to be far away already, far away like a runaway balloon, like a tiny *o* in the sky, so tiny-tiny you have to close your eyes to see it.

QUESTIONS FOR DISCUSSION

1. What does the author mean when she writes, "When you are eleven, you're also ten, and nine, and eight, and seven, and six . . ."?
2. Good description uses many of the five senses; identify parts of this essay where Cisneros does this.
3. How did this event change the writer?

QUESTIONS FOR WRITING

1. Write about an incident from your own education where you learned something. Make sure you describe what you were like before AND after the incident so that the reader can see the change.
2. Have you ever experienced a time when you were put down by fellow students—or co-workers, or other people you associate with? What happened? What was the effect?

Tiffany Stephenson—An Apology

Bjorn Skogquist

When I was in the fourth grade, I moved from a small Lutheran school of 100 to a larger publicly funded elementary school. Lincoln Elementary. Wow. Lincoln was a big school, full of a thousand different attitudes about everything from eating lunch to how to treat a new kid. It was a tough time for me, my first year, and more than anything, I wanted to belong.

Many things were difficult; the move my family had just made, trying to make new friends, settling into a new home, accepting a new stepfather. I remember crying a lot. I remember my parents fighting. They were having a difficult time with their marriage, and whether it was my stepfather's drinking, or my mother's stubbornness, it took an emotional toll on both me and my siblings. Despite all this, the thing that I remember most about the fourth grade is Tiffany Stephenson.

The first day of fourth grade at Lincoln Elementary School was an emptiness, and it felt enormous. I wasn't the only one who felt this way, but I was too absorbed in my own problems to notice anyone else's. I was upset that my father, my blood father, was in the hospital for abusing alcohol. Among other things, he was a schizophrenic. I was too young to understand these diseases, but I understood all too well that my daddy was very sick, and that I couldn't see him any more.

My first day at Lincoln was a very real moment in my life. The weather was both cloudy and intolerably sunny at the same time. Maybe it wasn't that the sun was so bright, maybe it was just that our eyes were still adjusted to morning shadows. It was one of those sequences that somehow stand out in my memory as unforgettable. I remember feeling gray inside. I think that all of us felt a little gray, and I would guess that most of us remember that first day as you might remember your grandmother's funeral, whether you liked it or not.

I walked in and sat near the back of the class, along with a few others. If you were different or weird or new, from another planet, you sat in the back because those were the only desks left. I sat at the far left of the room, in the back near the windows. For a while I just stared out into the playground, waiting for recess to come. Our teacher, Mrs. Bebow, came into the room and started talking to us. I don't remember exactly what she said that day, because I wasn't listening. I was numb to the world, concentrating solely on that playground. She seemed distant, far away, and I think that my whole day might have stayed numb if it weren't for a boy named Aaron Anderson.

Aaron, who sat to my right, leaned over and whispered, "My name's Aaron. And that's Tiffany Stephenson. Stay away from her. She's fat and ugly and she stinks." At that, a few others laughed, and I felt the numbness leaving me. Mrs. Bebow remarked that if we had something so terribly amusing to say, everyone had a right to know just what it was. Of course, we all quieted down. Then I asked which one was Tiffany, and Aaron pointed. There she was, coloring contentedly, sitting alone in the corner, in the very back, just like me. She was not fat or ugly, and as far as I knew, she didn't stink either. I even remember thinking that she was cute, but I quickly dismissed the thought because I already had a new friendship, even though it was in the common disgust of Tiffany Stephenson.

While all this was happening, our teacher Mrs. Bebow managed to take roll, after which she proceeded to lecture the boys on good behavior and then the girls on being young ladies. Every time she turned her back, airplanes and garbage flew across the room at Tiffany, along with a giggle, I don't think Tiffany Stephenson thought too much of us, that day or ever.

A few days later, one of the girls passed Tiffany a note. It ended up making her cry, and it got the girl a half an hour of detention. I was too busy trying to fit in to notice though, or didn't notice, or was afraid to notice, or simply didn't care.

That fall, both the boys and girls would go up to Tiffany on the playground and taunt her. They made absurd accusations, accusations about eating boogers at lunch, or about neglecting to wear underwear that day. Interestingly, this was the only activity that we participated in where a teacher didn't command, "OK, boys and girls need to partner up!" What we did to Tiffany Stephenson was mean, but in using her we all became common allies. I wonder if the teachers knew what we were up to when we made our next move, or if they thought that we were actually getting along. I think they knew at first, but we got craftier as time passed. And Tiffany had quit telling the teacher what happened. She knew that when we were ratted on, her taunts got worse. And they did get worse. We were mean, but we kept on because there was no one to stand out and say, "Enough."

When I think about that year, and about Tiffany, I remember that she was almost always alone. Toward the second half of the year, a retarded girl named Sharon Olsen befriended her. Sharon and Tiffany were a lot alike. They spent most of their time together coloring and drawing pictures, and those pictures always found their way to the prize board at the end of the week. The teacher knew that they needed a little encouragement, but mostly that "encouragement" ended up making us hate them more. We picked on Sharon a lot too, but not as much as we targeted Tiffany.

Through the long winter, our taunts became hateful jeers, and our threats of pushing and shoving became real acts. We carried our threats out against Tiffany, but with no real reason to hate her. A couple of times when we walked down to lunch, we even pushed her around the corner to an area under the stairs. We knew that if no other classes followed us, we could get away with our plan, which was to tease her until tears flowed. We always asked her if she was scared. She never gave us the right answer. In a quiet voice she would reply, "No. Now leave me alone." Sometimes we left her alone, and sometimes we just laughed. Tiffany must have felt so very scared and alone, but she had more than us, she had courage. We didn't care. The more we could scare her, the better, the closer, the stronger knit we somehow felt.

One afternoon, heading for lunch, a few of us stayed behind and blocked the doorway. Tiffany was there, alone again, and cornered by three boys. Looking back, I realized why we began pushing her around. We felt unbelievably close, so close to each other through our hatred. It was a feeling that I have experienced only a few times since. And not only was the experience ours to cherish, it was a delight for Mrs. Bebow's entire fourth grade class. We were a purpose that afternoon, and we knew it. Looking back to that moment, I feel more remorse for my coldness than I have felt for any other passing wrong. But then, there, I felt alive, unafraid, and strangely whole.

That afternoon changed me forever.

By the time we sent Tiffany Stephenson to the green linoleum, she was no longer a person. Her full name, given to her at birth as a loving gesture, was now a fat, smelly, ugly title. There, on the green linoleum of Mrs. Bebow's fourth grade classroom, amidst the decorations and smell of crayfish aquariums, Tiffany Stephenson received many kicks, punches and unkind words. We didn't kick or punch her very hard, and the things we said weren't especially foul, but they were inhuman. This event was the culmination of the inhumane hate and vengeance that had been growing inside of us all year long. And yet, if any one of us stopped for a second to look, to really take a good look at who it was lying there on the ground, curled up in a ball crying, we would have realized that she was one of us.

At the beginning of the year, all of us had felt like we were in the back of the room. We were all unknowns. But somehow during that year we had put ourselves above her by force, and I admit that for a long time I couldn't see my wrong. But I had wronged. I had caused someone pain for my own personal ambitions. I was now popular, and it was at Tiffany Stephenson's expense. I was a coward, stepping on her courage for one moment in the warm sunlight, above my own pale clouds.

Only recently do I realize my error. I wish I could have been the one to say, on that first fall afternoon, "Tiffany's not ugly, fat or stinky. She's just like you and me, and we're all here together." Really, I wish anyone would have said it. I know now that people need each other, and I wish I could tell the fourth grade that we could all be friends, that we could help each other with our problems. I wish that I could go back. But all I can do is apologize. So Tiffany, for all my shortcomings, and for sacrificing you for the sake of belonging, please forgive me.

QUESTIONS FOR DISCUSSION

1. Skogquist writes, "Only recently do I realize my error." Why do you think it took him so long to come to this realization?
2. Is the behavior of the students at Skogquist's school fairly typical? Why or why not?
3. How did the event at school change the author?

QUESTIONS FOR WRITING

1. Reflect on a time when you either bullied someone or were bullied by someone else. How do you view that event now?
2. Is bullying in schools a big problem? Should school officials take bullying more seriously?

Salvation

Langston Hughes

I was saved from sin when I was going on thirteen. But not really saved. It happened like this. There was a big revival at my Auntie Reed's church. Every night for weeks there had been much preaching, singing, praying, and shouting, and some very hardened sinners had been brought to Christ, and the membership of the church had grown by leaps and bounds. Then just before the revival ended, they had a special meeting for children, "to bring the young lambs to the fold." My aunt spoke of it for days ahead. That night I was escorted to the front row and placed on the mourners' bench with all the other young sinners, who had not yet been brought to Jesus.

My aunt told me that when you were saved you saw a light, and something happened to you inside! And Jesus came into your life! And God was with you from then on! She said you could see and hear and feel Jesus in your soul. I believed her. I had heard a great many old people say the same thing and it seemed to me they ought to know. So I sat there calmly in the hot, crowded church, waiting for Jesus to come to me.

The preacher preached a wonderful rhythmical sermon, all moans and shouts and lonely cries and dire pictures of hell, and then he sang a song about the ninety and nine safe in the fold, but one little lamb was left out in the cold. Then he said: "Won't you come? Won't you come to Jesus? Young lambs, won't you come?" And he held out his arms to all of us young sinners there on the mourners' bench. And the little girls cried. And some of them jumped up and went to Jesus right away. But most of us just sat there.

A great many old people came and knelt around us and prayed, old women with jet-black faces and braided hair, old men with work-gnarled hands. And the church sang a song about the lower lights are burning, some poor sinners to be saved. And the whole building rocked with prayer and song.

Still I kept waiting to *see* Jesus.

Finally all the young people had gone to the altar and were saved, but one boy and me. He was a rounder's son named Westley. Westley and I were surrounded by sisters and deacons praying. It was very hot in the church, and getting late now. Finally Westley said to me in a whisper: "God damn! I'm tired O' sitting here. Let's get up and be saved." So he got up and was saved.

Spare the Rod

Student Essay

When I was growing up during the 1950/1960's, parents raised their children by the biblical guideline that to "spare the rod" is to "spoil the child." Spanking was used to correct a whole spectrum of behavioral problems: being late home from school, stealing, telling lies, failing to do chores, getting poor grades, misbehaving in public, leaving food on the dinner plate. A child could expect to receive anything from a quick swat on the seat to a more carefully orchestrated whipping with a leather strap, depending on the severity of the "crime," and/or the anger of the parent. Although my own parents rarely hit me with anything more than a bare hand, I was spanked, and because my friends were also being reared the same way, it seemed natural. I fully expected that when I had children of my own I would also use this method, but by the time my son was five, I still had not been able to bring myself to deliver that first blow, and I feared that my son would grow to be a delinquent because of lack of proper discipline. However, the actions of my cousin at a family gathering helped me realize that my fears were unfounded, and that I should listen to the instincts which told me not to strike my child.

My cousin John is ten years my senior. A nationally ranked tennis player and minor celebrity, he had always found time for me, his constant shadow, and I had worshipped him. Tall, blond, tan, and successful, John was the golden athlete of our family, and he was well liked on the tennis circuit. His exuberance on and off the court and his ready smile in victory or defeat endeared everyone to him. However, he particularly earned my love and respect through his gentle and kind attitude toward me. When I was about five, I started going with John to his weekend tennis matches, often leaving very early in the morning and not returning till after dark. It must have been quite a responsibility having a precocious five-year-old tag along, one not many fifteen-year-olds would assume, but John was always patient. Whether he was explaining the nuances of the game of tennis, or admonishing me for my noisy enthusiasm during a match, he always assumed the role of patient guide. I learned to do as he asked out of a deep-seated desire to please him, and when I failed, my feelings of having disappointed John propelled me not to make the same mistake again. I missed all of my family when I left home, but I particularly missed John.

When I returned after a twelve year absence, my extended family, aunts, uncles, cousins, nieces and nephews, all gathered for a poolside barbecue. John was now the father of three children, but his looks had faded little over the years, and I thought that behind the good looking, though somewhat more severe face, still dwelt the kind, patient and gentle youth of my memory. I didn't spend much time with John because, in keeping with our family tradition, we soon divided into three distinct groups: the women seated in one corner casting watchful glances at their offspring, the men congregating around the perennial supply of beer, and the children scurrying in and out of the pool. But as the afternoon heat intensified, subtle changes occurred. The children became less patient at taking turns on the pool-slide, the women's watchful glances became steadfast glares as their offsprings' tempers began to fray, and the men became more vocal with each round of beer. My cousin's youngest son, who was about five years old, began to whine. His mother told him to stop but the whining persisted. The child probably should have been taken away somewhere quiet for a nap, but John had a better idea. An afternoon of drinking and telling tall tales had given him a florid-faced, arrogant, overbearing look, and as he called to his son, he started to unbuckle his belt.

The child was a quivering wreck as he approached his father, and his gentle whines soon changed to terrified shrieks as John inflicted blow after blow on the child's vulnerable bare legs. The whole ordeal couldn't have lasted more than a minute, but for me it seemed as though time stood still. I looked at my cousin towering above his young child and saw the ugly, contorted, enraged face of the adult and the frightened, pain-wracked face of the child. And as the sounds continued, images of other five-year-olds crept into my mind. I saw myself at that age being hit by my own father, and I felt the blows, the pain, and the humiliation as clearly as if the intervening years had not passed. Moreover, I vividly remembered my feelings toward my father when he was striking me: resentment, fear, betrayal, anger, powerlessness. And rather than feeling repentant after such punishment/discipline, I often felt a desire for revenge. One time, I dug up some of my father's newly-planted flowers to "get back" at him for hitting me.

In contrast with this image, I again saw myself as a five-year-old but this time at one of John's tennis matches. I had spent all day in the hot sun, and I wanted to leave. But John needed to wait so he could learn who his next opponent would be. In my anger at not getting my own way, I cut the strings on John's tennis racquet. He must have been furious, and he could have hit me; it would have been socially acceptable. Instead, he told me how he understood my tiredness, but that destroying the racquet, instead of hastening our departure, only prolonged the wait because now we had to find someone to restring the racquet. It took several hours, and during this period, my shame grew. I knew I had made a mistake, and I knew John was disappointed in me, but I also knew that I would not repeat my actions. The punishment for my action was that our departure was delayed, and I saw first-hand the consequences of my actions. I felt no resentment, humiliation, anger, fear, or betrayal, unless it was directed at myself. And I only wanted to correct my behavior, not get even with John.

And then I saw another five-year-old: my own son. With a look of horror, he watched the spectacle before us, and he asked me, "Mom, why is that man hurting the boy? Why don't we call the police?" Because my son was not familiar with the tenets of physical punishment, he saw the act as one of violence. He could see the defenseless position of the child, and his immediate reaction was that it should be stopped. And through my son's eyes, I too saw the situation clearly. John's son had been crying to start with, but now the crying had intensified. Simply put, the punishment had not worked; the child had not learned that whining at a barbecue is wrong. But he had learned other lessons. The first was that people who are bigger than he is and with more authority can hurt him, and he has no recourse. Sadly, the second lesson was that the role of a parent is one of aggression, power, and unyielding authority. And as my son moved into the protective circle of my arms, I knew those were lessons I never wanted him to learn.

As I held him, the cruel sounds stopped and, watching John's son run away, I wondered where he would find comfort. John passed me as he swaggered back to his group, but I could not look into his eyes. He was a stranger, someone I did not want to know. This was not the John of my childhood; where was that person now in this situation that was reminiscent of the summer afternoons we had spent together, when he had been, in one respect, my surrogate parent? I suspect that, like me, John felt that the role of being an effective parent required him to spank his children, and he suppressed the instincts that had guided him so well in dealing with my misbehavior. My cousin's wife, perhaps sensing my horror, said, "We want them to respect us." Respect! How could anyone respect someone who was inflicting such pain and public humiliation? But as a child I had respected John. I had respected his kindness; I had respected his understanding; I had respected his patience; most of all I had respected the fact that he considered me and my feelings enough NOT to publicly humiliate me. But my respect for John had just greatly diminished, and with the continuation of physical punishment, John's son would also respect his father less and less. I did not want this to happen between myself and my son and, as I held him, I knew that I would never strike him.

My son will be twenty this month and I have never raised my hand to him. He has grown to be a kind, gentle, compassionate young man, and without the threat of harsh punishment, the communication lines between us are always open and frequently used. We have even survived his teenage years with our relationship intact. I will never know if my choice to "spare the rod" is responsible for the way my son has turned out although I feel there is a correlation between the two. Unknowingly, John provided two parenting role models for me. The scene I witnessed at the barbecue depicted the stark reality of the style used by my own parents, and by examining my reaction to this scene—and to John—I was able to reject this method. But I was able to look back at my early relationship with John and see the kind of relationship I wanted to foster between myself and my son.

CHAPTER 5

Exemplification

EXEMPLIFICATION: USING EXAMPLES TO MAKE A POINT

As discussed in the chapter on Narration and Description, the use of vivid, specific details is essential in telling a good story, and good storytelling is one of the best ways to get a reader's attention. A good narrative essay depends upon the writer's ability to not simply "tell a story," but to **show** the reader the people, places, things, and events of the story so that the reader will be able to "see" the story and understand its significance. In keeping with this idea of "showing" vs. "telling," the exemplification (examples) essay is an essay in which the author supports his or her thesis with relevant, detailed, specific examples that clearly illustrate ("show") his or her points, and provides *analysis* that clearly ties the examples to the writer's thesis. Depending upon your topic, you will use examples that fall into one or more of the following categories:

- **Factual examples:** Factual, or "real life" examples, are examples that you might find in history, in the media, or in current events. When using factual examples, be sure to indicate the source of the example (see Richard Lederer's "English is a Crazy Language" for an example of the use of factual examples).

- **Personal Examples:** Personal examples are anecdotes taken from your own experiences and observations or the experiences and observations of someone you know. Remember to clearly indicate the source of the anecdote, and avoid making your essay one long personal narrative (See Brent Staples' "Black Men and Public Space" and Anna Quindlen's "Homeless" for excellent models of the use of personal examples).

- **Hypothetical Examples:** Hypothetical examples are examples you create to illustrate a particular point. Though they are fictional in the sense that they did not really happen, they should be situations that COULD, in theory, happen in the real world. Avoid basing the support for an essay entirely on hypothetical examples, as most readers expect at least some concrete factual support for an author's points (see Eve Golden's "Dangerous Curves" for an example of the use of hypothetical examples).

A Few Things to Remember When Writing the Exemplification Essay

- **Choose examples that are relevant to the topic and to your thesis.** The reader must be able to see the connection between the examples and your thesis. If the connection is not clear, the example should not be used. While it is usually necessary to provide some analysis to emphasize the connection between examples and the thesis, if an example requires too detailed of an explanation to make that connection clear, it may not be an appropriate example for the essay.

- **Provide a sufficient number of examples.** Depending upon the requirements set forth by your instructor, select examples that clearly and effectively illustrate your points to your reader. One example is generally not enough for a college-level essay; you should aim for at least TWO well-developed examples, perhaps more depending upon the page requirement and other guidelines indicated in your assignment.

- **Avoid making your examples long narratives.** Remember that the purpose of the exemplification essay is to use examples to illustrate points and to support a thesis, NOT to tell a story. While some examples, especially personal ones, will require some narrative and descriptive details, too much narration can cause your essay to stray from the topic, making it a narrative with no clear point instead of an exemplification essay.

- **Provide analysis to connect your examples to your thesis.** All good college essays must have *analysis*. Think of analysis as being a sort of "bridge" between your examples and your thesis—it explains how or why your examples support your thesis. Don't just present an example and leave it up to the reader to figure out how the example is relevant; remember your audience.

Black Men and Public Space

Brent Staples

My first victim was a woman—white, well dressed, probably in her late twenties. I came upon her late one evening on a deserted street in Hyde Park, a relatively affluent neighborhood in an otherwise mean, impoverished section of Chicago. As I swung onto the avenue behind her, there seemed to be a discreet, uninflammatory distance between us. Not so. She cast back a worried glance. To her, the youngish black man—a broad six feet two inches with a beard and billowing hair, both hands shoved into the pockets of a bulky military jacket—seemed menacingly close. After a few more quick glimpses, she picked up her pace and was soon running in earnest. Within seconds she disappeared into a cross street.

That was more than a decade ago. I was twenty-two years old, a graduate student newly arrived at the University of Chicago. It was in the echo of that terrified woman's footfalls that I first began to know the unwieldy inheritance I'd come into—the ability to alter public space in ugly ways. It was clear that she thought herself the quarry of a mugger, a rapist, or worse. Suffering a bout of insomnia, however, I was stalking sleep, not defenseless wayfarers. As a softy who is scarcely able to take a knife to a raw chicken—let alone hold one to a person's throat—I was surprised, embarrassed, and dismayed all at once. Her flight made me feel like an accomplice in tyranny. It also made it clear that I was indistinguishable from the muggers who occasionally seeped into the area from the surrounding ghetto. That first encounter, and those that followed, signified that a vast, unnerving gulf lay between nighttime pedestrians—particularly women—and me. And I soon gathered that being perceived as dangerous is a hazard in itself. I only needed to turn a corner into a dicey situation, or crowd some frightened, armed person in a foyer somewhere, or make an errant move after being pulled over by a policeman. Where fear and weapons meet—and they often do in urban America—there is always the possibility of death.

In that first year, my first away from my hometown, I was to become thoroughly familiar with the language of fear. At dark, shadowy intersections, I could cross in front of a car stopped at a traffic light and elicit the *thunk, thunk, thunk, thunk* of the driver—black, white, male, or female—hammering down the door locks. On less traveled streets after dark, I grew accustomed to but never comfortable with people crossing to the other side of the street rather than pass me. Then there were the standard unpleasantries with policemen, doormen, bouncers, cabdrivers, and others whose business it is to screen out troublesome individuals *before* there is any nastiness.

I moved to New York nearly two years ago and I have remained an avid night walker. In central Manhattan, the near-constant crowd cover minimizes tense one-on-one street encounters. Elsewhere—in SoHo, for example, where sidewalks are narrow and tightly spaced buildings shut out the sky—things can get very taut indeed.

After dark, on the warrenlike streets of Brooklyn where I live, I often see women who fear the worst from me. They seem to have set their faces on neutral, and with their purse straps strung across their chests bandolier-style, they forge ahead as though bracing themselves against being tackled. I understand, of course, that the danger they perceive is not a hallucination. Women are particularly vulnerable to street violence, and young black males are drastically overrepresented among the perpetrators of that violence. Yet these truths are no solace against the kind of alienation that comes of being ever the suspect, a fearsome entity with whom pedestrians avoid making eye contact.

It is not altogether clear to me how I reached the ripe old age of twenty-two without being conscious of the lethality nighttime pedestrians attributed to me. Perhaps it was because in Chester, Pennsylvania, the small, angry industrial town where I came of age in the 1960s, I was scarcely noticeable against a backdrop of gang warfare, street knifings, and murders. I grew up one of the good boys, had perhaps a half-dozen fistfights. In retrospect, my shyness of combat has clear sources.

As a boy, I saw countless tough guys locked away; I have since buried several, too. They were babies, really—a teenage cousin, a brother of twenty-two, a childhood friend in his mid-twenties—all gone down in episodes of bravado played out in the streets. I came to doubt the virtues of intimidation early on. I chose, perhaps unconsciously, to remain a shadow—timid, but a survivor.

The fearsomeness mistakenly attributed to me in public places often has a perilous flavor. The most frightening of these confusions occurred in the late 1970s and early 1980s, when I worked as a journalist in Chicago. One day, rushing into the office of a magazine I was writing for with a deadline story in hand, I was mistaken for a burglar. The office manager called security and, with an ad hoc posse, pursued me through the labyrinthine halls, nearly to my editor's door. I had no way of proving who I was. I could only move briskly toward the company of someone who knew me.

Another time I was on assignment for a local paper and killing time before an interview. I entered a jewelry store on the city's affluent Near North Side. The proprietor excused herself and returned with an enormous red Doberman pinscher straining at the end of a leash. She stood, the dog extended toward me, silent to my questions, her eyes bulging nearly out of her head. I took a cursory look around, nodded, and bade her good night.

Relatively speaking, however, I never fared as badly as another black male journalist. He went to nearby Waukegan, Illinois, a couple of summers ago to work on a story about a murderer who was born there. Mistaking the reporter for the killer, police officers hauled him from his car at gunpoint and but for his press credentials would probably have tried to book him. Such episodes are not uncommon. Black men trade tales like this all the time.

Over the years, I learned to smother the rage I felt at so often being taken for a criminal. Not to do so would surely have led to madness. I now take precautions to make myself less threatening. I move about with care, particularly late in the evening. I give a wide berth to nervous people on subway platforms during the wee hours, particularly when I have exchanged business clothes for jeans. If I happen to be entering a building behind some people who appear skittish, I may walk by, letting them clear the lobby before I return, so as not to seem to be following them. I have been calm and extremely congenial on those rare occasions when I've been pulled over by the police.

And on late-evening constitutionals I employ what has proved to be an excellent tension-reducing measure: I whistle melodies from Beethoven and Vivaldi and the more popular classical composers. Even steely New Yorkers hunching toward nighttime destinations seem to relax, and occasionally they even join in the tune. Virtually everybody seems to sense that a mugger wouldn't be warbling bright, sunny selections from Vivaldi's *Four Seasons*. It is my equivalent of the cowbell that hikers wear when they know they are in bear country.

QUESTIONS FOR DISCUSSION

1. Why does Staples refer to the woman at the beginning of the essay as "my first victim"?
2. What does Staples mean when he says that he has "the ability to alter public space in ugly ways"?
3. How does Staples deal with the problem he faces?

QUESTIONS FOR WRITING

1. Choose several of Staples' examples and discuss how he uses them to make his point.
2. At the end of the essay, Staples writes about the measures he takes to make others more comfortable around him. Do you agree with his choice to take these measures? Why or why not? Explain your answer.

Dangerous Curves

Eve Golden

My girlfriends and I spend an inordinate amount of time grousing about the terrible guys we fall for. So far the winner is Marie, who dated a guy who (1) lived in a trailer park because he liked it; (2) slept with a gun under the pillow; and (3) kept holy water in the freezer to *keep it holy longer.*

But—as the guys in my life are constantly making clear to me—men make the exact same mistakes, and fall for just as many of the wrong women. So in an effort to "C'mon, be fair about this, okay?" I've gone in search of *Five Women You Should Never Fall For.* . . . I spoke with Atlanta psychiatrist Frank Pittman, M.D., author of *Man Enough: Fathers, Sons and the Search for Masculinity.* After I described some of the terrible romances the men I know have wound up in, Dr. Pittman, who spends much time counseling couples with dysfunctional relationships, didn't let me down. "The women you mention are all Incomplete Women," he told me, making me feel nicely superior. "They seem safe to incomplete men," he added, thus explaining my current lack of social life: A complete, dangerous woman, that's me.

In fact, all of the women you're going to learn to avoid have some very attractive qualities, qualities that many men instinctively fall for. That's what makes it so critical for you to avoid them. So without further ado, let's meet our contestants in the Dating Game from Hell.

THE DAMSEL IN DISTRESS

She's the woman you see on those made-for-TV movies starring Barry Bostwick or Stephen Collins, about a good-natured guy who winds up entangled with some woman from the *Twilight Zone* (usually played by Meredith Baxter). She's helpless and heart-broken and just waiting for a big, strong man like you to come and sweep her off her feet. Does that sound a little anti-feminist, coming from a card-carrying NOW member? Remember, these women do exist. And they should all come equipped with big signs reading "Dangerous Curves Ahead."

"She is a disaster for everybody," Dr. Pittman states flat out. "Damsels in distress are never capable of knowing who is St. George and who is the dragon. If she is being abused by everyone in her life and you try to rescue her, I promise you it will only be a matter of time before you're seen as the next abuser."

My friend Rick agrees, having been the Stephen Collins character in one of those relationships. He tells me a sob story about his personal Damsel. "Ultimately, I stayed with her because she needed rescuing. I stuck around for a year and a half and never did rescue her. I learned from her, though: If there's a problem, get out early before it starts to affect your psyche."

How can you recognize the Damsel type? Dr. Pittman referees a lot of these relationships. "Any woman who falls in love with you too quickly, too desperately, too completely, must be nuts." Gee, there goes the plot of every movie made between 1929 and 1950. If you're married, you'll be able to spot her easily—she's the one making eyes at you from across the room. "These women are the sort of people who fall into affairs with married men," Dr. Pittman says. "Normal women don't do that." What makes a guy dumb enough to fall back? "A victim—a woman with more problems than you've got—will distract you from your problems. Briefly. Men are all too eager to believe that they're heroes, and that someone has finally noticed it." The lesson: Don't think too highly of yourself, and don't think too highly of anyone who thinks too highly of you.

THE (S)MOTHERER

You know how sometimes a man and a woman will have the exact same cold, yet the woman's up making hot tea and the man's in bed moaning, "Call a priest"? Some men just invite mothering, and some women (not me, not on your life) love playing Mama. Maybe 100 years ago, when women didn't have actual lives, that was a good way to vent emotional and physical energy. But nowadays, any woman who puts 100 percent of her hopes, dreams, fears and desires on her man's life rather than her own is not someone you need.

Dr. Pittman, of course, agrees. "A motherer doesn't require that you give anything back. She's so constantly giving that you end up feeling like a child." Surprisingly, this kind of woman still exists in the 1990s. I have to admit, I couldn't find any Big Mamas or their admirers around my New York digs, so I called my friend Norman, whose Deep-South sister is June Cleaver II. "Oh, she bought a vacuum cleaner for one boyfriend," says Norman. "She made payments on his truck, she did his laundry. He just ate it up."

You can see how this kind of relationship can be wonderful for a guy, at least for a while. But it can't be permanent. Eventually, you'll want to give something back, and she won't want what you have to offer. All she wants, Dr. Pittman says, is to live vicariously through you, and living two people's lives is a little bit more of a burden than most anyone would want to tackle. What ever happened to Norman's sister's boyfriend? "He got some other girl pregnant and married her," Norman says. "The guys who are attracted to my sister tend to be young and immature." Which reinforces my belief: that guys who fall for motherly types are entirely too much in touch with their inner child. Do us all a favor, will you, and get in touch with your inner adult?

THE CHAMELEON

You know the type: Suddenly she has a Boston accent, and suddenly she loves touch football, just because she's dating a Kennedy. "She's never an equal partner," Dr. Pittman says of this clinging vine, "because she gets her identity from adapting to the guy."

Oh, and I do know one or two chameleons. Very nice gals, but not with the best of self-images. Blanche was understandably defensive when I approached her on the topic, though she happily admitted that she indeed fit the bill. "I dress like my boyfriend. I think it's good," she says philosophically. "We can share clothes." Blanche went on to try and explain herself. "Guys' opinions and ways of doing things just rub off from being around them. It's an ego thing for them." But doesn't it show kind of a lack of ego on Blanche's part? So far, Blanche and her boyfriend seem happy, though she is starting to look more and more like him every day and everyone's pretty much hoping he doesn't start sporting a mustache.

Yet this type of one-sided relationship will eventually drag a man under. "The guy finds it flattering for a while, but neither the man nor the woman has the possibility of give-and-take, of being able to adapt to the other," Dr. Pittman says. "They naturally begin to feel something's missing." I talked to one of Blanche's ex-boyfriends, Max. Why did they break up? "We were just bored," he said. "We fell into a rut. Doing the same thing"—his thing, I might add—"night after night." Didn't the fact that Blanche brought nothing to the ball game have something to do with this? Max claimed not to know what I was talking about. "Well, yeah, we had a lot of the same interests, that's why we had such a great time together, isn't it?" I've known Blanche for years, I told him, and she was never the slightest bit interested in basketball, Van Damme films or Japanese food before they met. "Yeah?" His eyes light up; he's obviously delighted. "Well, I guess she got a few things out of the relationship, then, right?"

THE UPTOWN GIRL

You know her, or at least you've seen her: She's Sharon Stone, Geena Davis, whoever's on the cover of *Sports Illustrated* this year. Happily, most men don't go around shooting U.S. presidents to impress her. But it's hard not to fall for a woman who's just—let's face it—out of your league.

The most insidious thing about this unattainable glamour girl is that she thinks she's Just Folks. I tried to reach Sharon Stone, Drew Barrymore and Kelly Lynch for their opinions on the topic, but they proved to be, well, unattainable. I did, however, get my friend Lauren, a successful film producer, to comment. Lauren has natural red hair, looks like a more glamorous Jodie Foster, as sweet as you'd wish. But she started back in horror when I described her as Unattainable. "But I'm not!" she squealed, as a male friend rolled his eyes helplessly behind her. "I mean, I'm not gorgeous or anything like that!" She does admit that men seem afraid to approach her, but puts that down to shyness. She's utterly wrong. My not-too-terribly-shy friend Rick admits even he's intimidated by women like Lauren. "I just gaze at them with sheep eyes."

"There are women who just don't notice the guys who are pursuing them: that's what makes them unattainable," Dr. Pittman says. The men who pursue these glamorous ghosts "don't really want a woman. They're like dogs chasing cars. It's great exercise, as long as you know you'll never catch one. This is the perfect set-up for the guy who wants to be in love without all the problems of having a relationship. It's safe. Plus, he gets an identity from feeling the love he holds for her."

On the other hand, if you have normal, mutual relationships with other women, there's nothing wrong with having a crush on someone now and then. Dr. Pittman sheepishly admits that "I have that relationship with Susan Sarandon—whom I've never met, of course."

THE CRUISE DIRECTOR

Okay, I have a confession. When my editor described this kind of Woman to Avoid, I thought he was being sarcastic and describing me: opinionated, always in control, bossy, having to make all the plans and double-check them afterward. This type of woman may be nerve-racking, but I hasten to add she always gets her stories in on deadline.

"She sounds real nice," agrees Dr. Pittman. "I have entirely too many pleasures in life to waste time running my life. I prefer having someone else do it for me. A Cruise Director can be someone who frees you up to be successful, to be creative."

That's fine as long as you're happy to leave your social life up to someone else's whims, and as long as she's willing to play cruise director for an extended tour. But it doesn't always work out that way. My friend Walter refused to talk about his ex-wife, but his new wife, Carol, was delighted to help. "Oh, she was such a pushy type," Carol enthused. "She ran everything, which was fun for both of them, at least for a while. But then the challenge was over, and she and Walter split up." Dr. Pittman says there can indeed be downsides to dating a Cruise Director. "If you're scared of women and you've got one who runs your life, you're going to feel controlled, that your autonomy is impinged upon, like an adolescent.

She's for a guy who's got something to do that's more important than proving that women can't tell him what to do. But for the guy who's scared of female control, she'd be a disaster."

So maybe you're smart enough to avoid the above bachelorettes. Or maybe you're the type who clings to one after the other like Tarzan swinging through the vines. What's Dr. Pittman's advice for guys who keep falling for the wrong woman? "Get into a permanent, full-time committed relationship with someone with whom you don't get along terribly well and are basically incompatible." Yikes! He continues: "That puts you in the position of having to constantly examine yourself, develop new skills, learn to see the world from another perspective—it's a great maturing process." So is running away to join the circus, but I wouldn't recommend it for everyone.

"Seriously," Dr. Pittman explains, "you need incompatibility in a relationship. Of course, you need compatibility, too—to make you feel comfortable, safe, understood. But compatibility is never complete, and never permanent. It takes a certain amount of conflict to give a relationship life."

If that's the hard way, here's the easy one: Guys, if you want to have a relationship in the worst way, take it from me, you will. There's this odd notion today that if you're not involved in a romantic/sexual relationship, you're somehow half a person and cannot possibly be happy.

Bull. How many hours have you spent on the phone with friends, moaning to your barkeep or to your therapist about how unhappy you are in one relationship or another? Take my advice and think long and hard next time you fall. As my wise old Aunt Ida once told me, "It's better to be alone than to wish you were."

QUESTIONS FOR DISCUSSION

1. What is the author's purpose in writing the essay?
2. What are some of the "attractive qualities" the author warns men to avoid?
3. Why does Dr. Pittman say "you need incompatibility in a relationship"?

QUESTIONS FOR WRITING

1. What advice would you give to people who are dating/looking for a relationship? Explain your "do's" and "don'ts" of relationships, providing examples to illustrate your points.
2. What types of people make good friends? What types of people should be avoided? Using examples, illustrate several different types of people who make good friends and those who do not.

Homeless

Anna Quindlen

Her name was Ann, and we met in the Port Authority Bus Terminal several Januarys ago. I was doing a story on homeless people. She said I was wasting my time talking to her; she was just passing through, although she'd been passing through for more than two weeks. To prove to me that this was true, she rummaged through a tote bag and a manila envelope and finally unfolded a sheet of typing paper and brought out her photographs.

They were not pictures of family, or friends, or even a dog or cat, its eyes brown-red in the flashbulb's light. They were pictures of a house. It was like a thousand houses in a hundred towns, not suburb, not city, but somewhere in between, with aluminum siding and a chain-link fence, a narrow driveway running up to a one-car garage and a patch of backyard. The house was yellow. I looked on the back for a date or a name, but neither was there. There was no need for discussion. I knew what she was trying to tell me, for it was something I had often felt. She was not adrift, alone, anonymous, although her bags and her raincoat with the grime shadowing its creases had made me believe she was. She had a house, or at least once upon a time had had one. Inside were curtains, a couch, a stove, potholders. You are where you live. She was somebody.

I've never been very good at looking at the big picture, taking the global view, and I've always been a person with an overactive sense of place, the legacy of an Irish grandfather. So it is natural that the thing that seems most wrong with the world to me right now is that there are so many people with no homes. I'm not simply talking about shelter from the elements, or three square meals a day or a mailing address to which the welfare people can send the check—although I know that all these are important for survival. I'm talking about a home, about precisely those kinds of feelings that have wound up in cross-stitch and French knots on samplers over the years.

Home is where the heart is. There's no place like it. I love my home with a ferocity totally out of proportion to its appearance or location. I love dumb things about it: the hot-water heater, the plastic rack you drain dishes in, the roof over my head, which occasionally leaks. And yet it is precisely those dumb things that make it what it is—a place of certainty, stability, predictability, privacy, for me and for my family. It is where I live. What more can you say about a place than that? That is everything.

Yet it is something that we have been edging away from gradually during my lifetime and the lifetimes of my parents and grandparents. There was a time when where you lived often was where you worked and where you grew the food you ate and even where you were buried. When that era passed, where you lived at least was where your parents had lived and where you would live with your children when you became enfeebled. Then, suddenly where you lived was where you lived for three years, until you could move on to something else and something else again.

And so we have come to something else again, to children who do not understand what it means to go to their rooms because they have never had a room, to men and women whose fantasy is a wall they can paint a color of their own choosing, to old people reduced to sitting on molded plastic chairs, their skin blue-white in the lights of a bus station, who pull pictures of houses out of their bags. Homes have stopped being homes. Now they are real estate.

People find it curious that those without homes would rather sleep sitting up on benches or huddled in doorways than go to shelters. Certainly some prefer to do so because they are emotionally ill, because they have been locked in before and they are damned if they will be locked in again. Others are afraid of the violence and trouble they may find there. But some seem to want something that is not available in shelters, and they will not compromise, not for a cot, or oatmeal, or a shower, with special soap that kills the bugs. "One room," a woman with a baby who was sleeping on her sister's floor, once told me, "painted blue." That was the crux of it; not size or location, but pride of ownership. Painted blue.

This is a difficult problem, and some wise and compassionate people are working hard at it. But in the main I think we work around it, just as we walk around it when it is lying on the sidewalk or sitting in the bus terminal—the problem, that is. It has been customary to take people's pain and lessen our own participation in it by turning it into an issue, not a collection of human beings. We turn an adjective into a noun: the poor, not poor people; the homeless, not Ann or the man who lives in the box or the woman who sleeps on the subway grate.

Sometimes I think we would be better off if we forgot about the broad strokes and concentrated on the details. Here is a woman without a bureau. There is a man with no mirror, no wall to hang it on. They are not the homeless. They are people who have no homes. No drawer that holds the spoons. No window to look out upon the world. My God. That is everything.

QUESTIONS FOR DISCUSSION

1. Why does Quindlen include the story of Ann, the woman she met in the bus terminal?
2. How, according to Quindlen, has the concept of "home" changed over the years?

3. Quindlen points out that "we turn an adjective into a noun; the poor, not poor people, the homeless, not Ann or the man who lives in the box or the woman who sleeps on the subway grate." What does she mean?

QUESTIONS FOR WRITING

1. In the final paragraph of Quindlen's essay, she writes, "Sometimes I think we would be better off if we forgot about the broad strokes and concentrated on the details." Explain the significance of the final paragraph, and explain YOUR response to Quindlen's point.
2. Discuss the significance of the concept of "home." You may use points and examples from Quindlen's essay, but you should also discuss your OWN ideas, observations, or experiences.

On Compassion

Barbara Lazear Ascher

The man's grin is less the result of circumstance than dreams or madness. His buttonless shirt, with one sleeve missing, hangs outside the waist of his baggy trousers. Carefully plaited dreadlocks bespeak a better time, long ago. As he crosses Manhattan's Seventy-ninth Street, his gait is the shuffle of the forgotten ones held in place by gravity rather than plans. On the corner of Madison Avenue, he stops before a blond baby in an Aprica stroller. The baby's mother waits for the light to change and her hands close tighter on the stroller's handle as she sees the man approach.

The others on the corner, five men and women waiting for the crosstown bus, look away. They daydream a bit and gaze into the weak rays of November light. A man with a briefcase lifts and lowers the shiny toe of his right shoe, watching the light reflect, trying to catch and balance it, as if he could hold and make it his, to ease the heavy gray of coming January, February, and March. The winter months that will send snow around the feet, calves, and knees of the grinning man as he heads for the shelter of Grand Central or Pennsylvania Station.

But for now, in this last gasp of autumn warmth, he is still. His eyes fix on the baby. The mother removes her purse from her shoulder and rummages through its contents: lipstick, a lace handkerchief, an address book. She finds what she's looking for and passes a folded dollar over her child's head to the man who stands and stares even though the light has changed and traffic navigates about his hips.

His hands continue to dangle at his sides. He does not know his part. He does not know that acceptance of the gift and gratitude are what make this transaction complete. The baby, weary of the unwavering stare, pulls its blanket over its head. The man does not look away. Like a bridegroom waiting at the altar, his eyes pierce the white veil.

The mother grows impatient and pushes the stroller before her, bearing the dollar like a cross. Finally, a black hand rises and closes around green.

Was it fear or compassion that motivated the gift?

Up the avenue, at Ninety-first Street, there is a small French bread shop where you can sit and eat a buttery, overpriced croissant and wash it down with rich cappuccino. Twice when I have stopped here to stave hunger or stay the cold, twice as I have sat and read and felt the warm rush of hot coffee and milk, an old man has wandered in and stood inside the entrance. He wears a stained blanket pulled up to his chin, and a woolen hood pulled down to his gray, bushy eyebrows. As he stands, the scent of stale cigarettes and urine fills the small, overheated room.

The owner of the shop, a moody French woman, emerges from the kitchen with steaming coffee in a Styrofoam cup, and a small paper bag of . . . of what? Yesterday's bread? Today's croissant? He accepts the offering as silently as he came, and is gone.

Twice I have witnessed this, and twice I have wondered, what compels this woman to feed this man? Pity? Care? Compassion? Or does she simply want to rid her shop of his troublesome presence? If expulsion were her motivation she would not reward his arrival with gifts of food. Most proprietors do not. They chase the homeless from their midst with expletives and threats.

As winter approaches, the mayor of New York City is moving the homeless off the streets and into Bellevue Hospital. The New York Civil Liberties Union is watchful. They question whether the rights of these people who live in our parks and doorways are being violated by involuntary hospitalization.

I think the mayor's notion is humane, but I fear it is something else as well. Raw humanity offends our sensibilities. We want to protect ourselves from an awareness of rags with voices that make no sense and scream forth in inarticulate rage. We do not wish to be reminded of the tentative state of our own well-being and sanity. And so, the troublesome presence is removed from the awareness of the electorate.

Like other cities, there is much about Manhattan now that resembles Dickensian London. Ladies in high-heeled shoes pick their way through poverty and madness. You hear more cocktail party complaints than usual, "I just can't take New York anymore." Our citizens dream of the open spaces of Wyoming, the manicured exclusivity of Hobe Sound.

And yet, it may be that these are the conditions that finally give birth to empathy, the mother of compassion. We cannot deny the existence of the helpless as their presence grows. It is impossible to insulate ourselves against what is at our very doorstep. I don't believe that one is born compassionate. Compassion is not a character trait like a sunny disposition. It must be learned, and it is learned by having adversity at our windows, coming through the gates of our yards, the walls of our towns, adversity that becomes so familiar that we begin to identify and empathize with it.

For the ancient Greeks, drama taught and reinforced compassion within a society. The object of Greek tragedy was to inspire empathy in the audience so that the common response to the hero's fall was: "There, but for the grace of God, go I." Could it be that this was the response of the mother who offered the dollar, the French woman who gave the food? Could it be that the homeless, like those ancients, are reminding us of our common humanity? Of course, there is a difference. This play doesn't end—and the players can't go home.

QUESTIONS FOR DISCUSSION

1. What is the author's thesis?
2. What purpose do the author's examples serve?
3. Where, according to Ascher, does compassion originate?

QUESTIONS FOR WRITING

1. In paragraph 6, Ascher asks, "Was it fear or compassion that motivated the gift?" Discuss possible motivations for giving (or NOT giving) to the homeless. You should support your discussion with specific, factual examples and examples from your own observations and experiences.
2. In paragraph 3, Ascher argues that "Compassion is not a character trait like a sunny disposition." What do you think? Discuss your response to Ascher's point. Be sure to explain what compassion means to you and how you think people come to exhibit compassion. Provide specific examples, factual and/or personal, to support your points.

English Is a Crazy Language

Richard Lederer

English is the most widely spoken language in the history of our planet, used in some way by at least one out of every seven human beings around the globe. Half of the world's books are written in English, and the majority of international telephone calls are made in English. English is the language of over sixty percent of the world's radio programs, many of them beamed, ironically, by the Russians, who know that to win friends and influence nations, they're best off using English. More than seventy percent of international mail is written and addressed in English, and eighty percent of all computer text is stored in English. English has acquired the largest vocabulary of all the world's languages, perhaps as many as two million words, and has generated one of the noblest bodies of literature in the annals of the human race.

Nonetheless, it is now time to face the fact that English is a crazy language.

In the crazy English language, the blackbird hen is brown, blackboards can be blue or green, and blackberries are green and then red before they are ripe. Even if blackberries were really black and blueberries really blue, what are strawberries, cranberries, elderberries, huckleberries, raspberries, boysenberries, mulberries, and gooseberries supposed to look like?

To add to the insanity, there is no butter in buttermilk, no egg in eggplant, no grape in grapefruit, neither worms nor wood in wormwood, neither pine nor apple in pineapple, neither peas nor nuts in peanuts, and no ham in a hamburger. (In fact, if somebody invented a sandwich consisting of a ham patty in a bun, we would have a hard time finding a name for it.) To make matters worse, English muffins weren't invented in England, french fries in France, or danish pastries in Denmark. And we discover even more culinary madness in the revelations that sweetmeat is candy, while sweetbread, which isn't sweet, is made from meat.

In this unreliable English tongue, greyhounds aren't always grey (or gray); panda bears and koala bears aren't bears (they're marsupials); a woodchuck is a groundhog, which is not a hog; a horned toad is a lizard; glowworms are fireflies, but fireflies are not flies (they're beetles); ladybugs and lightning bugs are also beetles (and to propagate, a significant proportion of ladybugs must be male); a guinea pig is neither a pig nor from Guinea (it's a South American rodent); and a titmouse is neither mammal nor mammaried.

Language is like the air we breathe. It's invisible, inescapable, indispensable, and we take it for granted. But when we take the time, step back, and listen to the sounds that escape from the holes in people's faces and explore the paradoxes and vagaries of English, we find that hot dogs can be cold, darkrooms can be lit, homework can be done in school, nightmares can take place in broad daylight, while morning sickness and daydreaming can take place at night, tomboys are girls, midwives can be men, hours—especially happy hours and rush hours—can last longer than sixty minutes, quicksand works *very* slowly, boxing rings are square, silverware can be made of plastic and tablecloths of paper, most telephones are dialed by being punched (or pushed?), and most bathrooms don't have any baths in them. In fact, a dog can go to the bathroom under a tree—no bath, no room; it's still going to the bathroom. And doesn't it seem at least a little bizarre that we go to the bathroom in order to go to the bathroom?

Why is it that a woman can man a station but a man can't woman one, that a man can father a movement but a woman can't mother one, and that a king rules a kingdom but a queen doesn't rule a queendom? How did all those Renaissance men reproduce when there don't seem to have been any Renaissance women?

A writer is someone who writes, and a stinger is something that stings. But fingers don't fing, grocers don't groce, hammers don't ham, and humdingers don't humding. If the plural of *tooth is teeth*, shouldn't the plural of *booth* be *beeth?* One goose, two geese—so one moose, two meese? One index, two indices—one Kleenex, two Kleenices? If people ring a bell today and rang a bell yesterday, why don't we say that they flang a ball? If they wrote a letter, perhaps they also bote their tongue. If the teacher taught, why isn't it also true that the preacher praught? Why is it that the sun shone yesterday while I shined my shoes, that I treaded water and then trod on soil, and that I flew out to see a World Series game in which my favorite player flied out?

If we conceive a conception and receive at a reception, why don't we grieve a greption and believe a beleption? If a horsehair mat is made from the hair of horses and a camel's hair brush from the hair of camels, from what is a mohair coat made? If a vegetarian eats vegetables, what does a humanitarian eat? If a firefighter fights fire, what does a freedom fighter fight? If a weightlifter lifts weights, what does a shoplifter lift? If *pro* and *con* are opposites, is congress the opposite of progress?

Sometimes you have to believe that all English speakers should be committed to an asylum for the verbally insane. In what other language do people drive in a parkway and park in a driveway? In what other language do people recite at a play and play at a recital? In what other language do privates eat in the general mess and generals eat in the private mess? In what other language do men get hernias and women get hysterectomies? In what other language do people ship by truck and send cargo by ship? In what other language can your nose run and your feet smell?

How can a slim chance and a fat chance be the same, "what's going on?" and "what's coming off?" be the same, and a bad licking and a good licking be the same, while a wise man and a wise guy are opposites? How can sharp speech and blunt speech be the same and *quite a lot* and *quite a few* the same, while *overlook* and *oversee* are opposites? How can the weather be hot as hell one day and cold as hell the next?

If *button* and *unbutton* and *tie* and *untie* are opposites, why are *loosen* and *unloosen* and *ravel* and *unravel* the same? If *bad* is the opposite of *good, hard* the opposite of *soft,* and *up* the opposite of *down,* why are *badly* and *goodly, hardly* and *softly,* and *upright* and *downright* not opposing pairs? If harmless actions are the opposite of harmful actions, why are shameless and shameful behavior the same and pricey objects less expensive than priceless ones? If appropriate and inappropriate remarks and passable and impassable mountain trails are opposites, why are flammable and inflammable materials, heritable and inheritable property, and passive and impassive people the same and valuable objects less treasured than invaluable ones? If *uplift* is the same as *lift up,* why are *upset* and *set up* opposite in meaning? Why are *pertinent* and *impertinent, canny* and *uncanny,* and *famous* and *infamous* neither opposites nor the same? How can *raise* and *raze* and *reckless* and *wreckless* be opposites when each pair contains the same sound?

Why is it that when the sun or the moon or the stars are out, they are visible, but when the lights are out, they are invisible, and that when I wind up my watch, I start it, but when I wind up this essay, I shall end it?

English is a crazy language.

QUESTIONS FOR DISCUSSION

1. Why, according to Lederer, is English a "crazy language"?
2. Lederer says that English is "unreliable" – why?
3. Why is English such an important language?

QUESTIONS FOR WRITING

1. In paragraph 10, Lederer writes, "Sometimes you have to believe that all English speakers should be committed to an asylum for the verbally insane." Based on what you have read in Lederer's essay and what you have experienced, do you agree? Explain your answer, using points from the essay and your own ideas, observations, and experiences.
2. Can you think of any other examples that illustrate the claim that "English is a crazy language"? Support a point similar to Lederer's, using examples and observations from your own experiences as an English-language speaker (whether you are a native speaker of English or English is your second language). You might, for example, focus on clichés, idiomatic expressions, or current slang.

CHAPTER 6

Comparison and Contrast

COMPARISON AND CONTRAST: EXAMINING SIMILARITIES AND DIFFERENCES

You need a new car. How do you decide which car to buy? Chances are that you don't walk into the nearest auto dealer and purchase the first car you come across. You probably begin looking at lots of cars, narrow it down to two or three, and then closely examine what each car has to offer in relation to the others. You are comparing and contrasting. Comparing means examining similarities and contrasting means examining the differences.

You may have written comparison/contrast essays in high school, and this is a very useful skill to have for writing college essays. For instance, your history teacher may ask you to compare/contrast the period before the Civil War with the period afterwards. Or your political science teacher may ask you to decide whether George Washington or Abraham Lincoln was the better president; you will need to compare/contrast the two presidents to decide. With a little guidance, comparison/contrast is fairly easy to write, but in order to write **GOOD** comparison/contrast, keep the following in mind. A comparison/contrast essay should

- **Have a purpose:** An essay that merely aims to show how two things are alike and how they are different is probably not going to engage and maintain your reader's interest, so make sure there is a purpose for the comparison. An essay about pre and post Civil War periods will be more interesting if it has something to say about the similarities and/or differences: In which period were people happier? Which period had a greater influence on our present economic situation? Was America better off after the Civil War? One good purpose is to argue that one object is better than or preferable to another. If you develop your thesis with this purpose in mind, you will have a position to prove—always a much more interesting essay.

- **Have important points of comparison:** Say you are trying to decide whether to go to college in a large city (San Francisco) or in a smaller town (Davis). Some logical points to consider for each might be
  - Cost of Living
  - Job Opportunities
  - Entertainment
  - Choice of schools

- **Be logically organized:** You have selected your subjects for comparison/contrast and have now decided on the important points of comparison. There are two common structures for composing comparison/contrast essays:
  - Subject by subject
  - Point by point

- **Subject by Subject:**
  If you are going to arrange the details in subject by subject order, you would structure your essay this way.
  San Francisco
  > Cost of living
  > Job opportunities
  > Entertainment
  > Choice of schools
  Davis
  > Cost of Living
  > Job opportunities
  > Entertainment
  > Choice of schools

The biggest drawback to this structure is that in a long essay, your readers may have forgotten everything you say about San Francisco when they get to the part about Davis. This method of organization is best suited for short essays.

- **Point by point:**
  If you arrange the details in point by point order, they would appear as follows.
  Cost of living
  > San Francisco
  > Davis

  Job opportunities
  > San Francisco
  > Davis

  Entertainment
  > San Francisco
  > Davis

> Choice of schools
> San Francisco
> Davis

The biggest drawback to this structure is that your reader may feel as though he/she is at a tennis match—sitting at the net—with his/her head moving backwards and forwards at a rapid pace. You'll need to make sure you use good transitions (See Chapter 1) to help make the connections between points smooth.

After you become more practiced at writing comparison/contrast, you will probably combine these two methods of organization so that your essay doesn't sound too mechanical. Notice in "Conversational Ballgames," how Sakamoto mixed up the two methods.

- **Be consistent and have balance:**
  - If you're going to write about one point for the first subject, make sure you also discuss this point for the second.
  - Without being too rigorous, try to achieve fairly good balance between points and subjects. Don't for instance spend three pages talking about San Francisco and only one about Davis.

Neat People vs. Sloppy People

Suzanne Britt

I've finally figured out the difference between neat people and sloppy people. The distinction is, as always, moral. Neat people are lazier and
meaner than sloppy people.

Sloppy people, you see, are not really sloppy. Their sloppiness is
merely the unfortunate consequence of their extreme moral rectitude.
Sloppy people carry in their mind's eye a heavenly vision, a precise
plan, that is so stupendous, so perfect, it can't be achieved in this world
or the next.

Sloppy people live in Never-Never Land. Someday is their métier.
Someday they are planning to alphabetize all their books and set up home
catalogs. Someday they will go through their wardrobes and mark certain
items for tentative mending and certain items for passing on to relatives
of similar shape and size. Someday sloppy people will make family scrap-
books into which they will put newspaper clippings, postcards, locks of
hair, and the dried corsage from their senior prom. Someday they will file
everything on the surface of their desks, including the cash receipts from
coffee purchases at the snack shop. Someday they will sit down and read
all the back issues of the *New Yorker.*

For all these noble reasons and more, sloppy people never get neat.
They aim too high and wide. They save everything, planning someday to
file, order, and straighten out the world. But while these ambitious plans
take clearer and clearer shape in their heads, the books spill from the
shelves onto the floor, the clothes pile up in the hamper and closet, the
family mementos accumulate in every drawer, the surface of the desk is
buried under mounds of paper and the unread magazines threaten to
reach the ceiling.

Sloppy people can't bear to part with anything. They give loving attention to every detail. When sloppy people say they're going to tackle the
surface of the desk, they really mean it. Not a paper will go unturned; not
a rubber band will go unboxed. Four hours or two weeks into the excava-
tion, the desk looks exactly the same, primarily because the sloppy person
is meticulously creating new piles of papers with new headings and
scrupulously stopping to read all the old book catalogs before he throws
them away. A neat person would just bulldoze the desk.

Neat people are bums and clods at heart. They have cavalier attitudes toward possessions, including family heirlooms. Everything is just
another dustcatcher to them. If anything collects dust, it's got to go and

that's that. Neat people will toy with the idea of throwing the children out of the house just to cut down on the clutter.

Neat people don't care about process. They like results. What they want to do is get the whole thing over with so they can sit down and watch the rasslin' on TV. Neat people operate on two unvarying principles: Never handle any item twice, and throw everything away.

The only thing messy in a neat person's house is the trash can. The minute something comes to a neat person's hand, he will look at it, try to decide if it has immediate use and, finding none, throw it in the trash.

Neat people are especially vicious with mail. They never go through their mail unless they are standing directly over a trash can. If the trash can is beside the mailbox, even better. All ads, catalogs, pleas for charitable contributions, church bulletins and money-saving coupons go straight into the trash can without being opened. All letters from home, postcards from Europe, bills and pay-checks are opened, immediately responded to, then dropped in the trash can. Neat people keep their receipts only for tax purposes. That's it. No sentimental salvaging of birthday cards or the last letter a dying relative ever wrote. Into the trash it goes.

Neat people place neatness above everything, even economics. They are incredibly wasteful. Neat people throw away several toys every time they walk through the den. I knew a neat person once who threw away a perfectly good dish drainer because it had mold on it. The drainer was too much trouble to wash. And neat people sell their furniture when they move. They will sell a La-Z-Boy recliner while you are reclining in it.

Neat people are no good to borrow from. Neat people buy everything in expensive little single portions. They get their flour and sugar in two-pound bags. They wouldn't consider clipping a coupon, saving a leftover, reusing plastic nondairy whipped cream containers or rinsing off tin foil and draping it over the unmoldy dish drainer. You can never borrow a neat person's newspaper to see what's playing at the movies. Neat people have the paper all wadded up and in the trash by 7:05 A.M.

Neat people cut a clean swath through the organic as well as the inorganic world. People, animals, and things are all one to them. They are so insensitive. After they've finished with the pantry, the medicine cabinet, and the attic, they will throw out the red geranium (too many leaves), sell the dog (too many fleas), and send the children off to boarding school (too many scuffmarks on the hard-wood floors).

QUESTIONS FOR DISCUSSION

1. Is the structure of this essay "point by point" or "subject by subject"?
2. What is the significance of the sentence, "A neat person would just bulldoze the desk?"
3. Do you think Suzanne Britt is a "neat" or "sloppy" person? Explain.

QUESTIONS FOR WRITING

1. Using Britt's "evidence," do you consider yourself a neat or a sloppy person?
2. Does Britt provide an accurate depiction of neat and sloppy people? Why or why not? Use evidence from the essay as well as from your own experiences and observations.

Conversational Ballgames

Nancy Masterson Sakamoto

After I was married and had lived in Japan for a while, my Japanese gradually improved to the point where I could take part in simple conversations with my husband and his friends and family. And I began to notice that often, when I joined in, the others would look startled, and the conversational topic would come to a halt. After this happened several times, it became clear to me that I was doing something wrong. But for a long time, I didn't know what it was.

Finally, after listening carefully to many Japanese conversations, I discovered what my problem was. Even though I was speaking Japanese, I was handling the conversation in a western way.

Japanese-style conversations develop quite differently from western-style conversations. And the difference isn't only in the languages. I realized that just as I kept trying to hold western-style conversations even when I was speaking Japanese, so my English students kept trying to hold Japanese-style conversations even when they were speaking English. We were unconsciously playing entirely different conversational ballgames.

A western-style conversation between two people is like a game of tennis. If I introduce a topic, a conversational ball, I expect you to hit it back. If you agree with me, I don't expect you simply to agree and do nothing more. I expect you to add something—a reason for agreeing, another example, or an elaboration to carry the idea further. But I don't expect you always to agree. I am just as happy if you question me, or challenge me, or completely disagree with me. Whether you agree or disagree, your response will return the ball to me.

And then it is my turn again. I don't serve a new ball from my original starting line. I hit your ball back again from where it has bounced. I carry your idea further, or answer your questions or objections, or challenge or question you. And so the ball goes back and forth, with each of us doing our best to give it a new twist, an original spin, or a powerful smash.

And the more vigorous the action, the more interesting and exciting the game. Of course, if one of us gets angry, it spoils the conversation, just as it spoils a tennis game. But getting excited is not at all the same as getting angry. After all, we are not trying to hit each other. We are trying to hit the ball. So long as we attack only each other's opinions, and do not attack each other personally, we don't expect anyone to get hurt. A good conversation is supposed to be interesting and exciting.

If there are more than two people in the conversation, then it is like doubles in tennis, or like volleyball. There's no waiting in line. Whoever is nearest and quickest hits the ball, and if you step back, someone else will hit it. No one stops the game to give you a turn. You're responsible for taking your own turn.

But whether it's two players or a group, everyone does his best to keep the ball going, and no one person has the ball for very long.

A Japanese-style conversation, however, is not at all like tennis or volleyball. It's like bowling. You wait for your turn. And you always know your place in line. It depends on such things as whether you are older or younger, a close friend or a relative stranger to the previous speaker, in a senior or junior position, and so on.

When your turn comes, you step up to the starting line with your bowling ball, and carefully bowl it. Everyone else stands back and watches politely, murmuring encouragement. Everyone waits until the ball has reached the end of the alley, and watches to see if it knocks down all the pins, or only some of them, or none of them. There is a pause, while everyone registers your score.

Then, after everyone is sure that you have completely finished your turn, the next person in line steps up to the same starting line, with a different ball. He doesn't return your ball, and he does not begin from where your ball stopped. There is no back and forth at all. All the balls run parallel. And there is always a suitable pause between turns. There is no rush, no excitement, no scramble for the ball.

No wonder everyone looked startled when I took part in Japanese conversations. I paid no attention to whose turn it was, and kept snatching the ball halfway down the alley and throwing it back at the bowler. Of course the conversation died. I was playing the wrong game.

This explains why it is almost impossible to get a western-style conversation or discussion going with English students in Japan. I used to think that the problem was their lack of English language ability. But I finally came to realize that the biggest problem is that they, too, are playing the wrong game.

Whenever I serve a volleyball, everyone just stands back and watches it fall, with occasional murmurs of encouragement. No one hits it back. Everyone waits until I call on someone to take a turn. And when that person speaks, he doesn't hit my ball back. He serves a new ball. Again, everyone just watches it fall.

So I call on someone else. This person does not refer to what the previous speaker has said. He also serves a new ball. Nobody seems to have paid any attention to what anyone else has said. Everyone begins again from the same starting line, and all the balls run parallel. There is never any back and forth. Everyone is trying to bowl with a volleyball.

And if I try a simpler conversation, with only two of us, then the other person tries to bowl with my tennis ball. No wonder foreign English teachers in Japan get discouraged.

Now that you know about the difference in the conversational ball-games, you may think that all your troubles are over. But if you have been trained all your life to play one game, it is no simple matter to switch to another, even if you know the rules. Knowing the rules is not at all the same thing as playing the game.

Even now, during a conversation in Japanese I will notice a startled reaction, and belatedly realize that once again I have rudely interrupted by instinctively trying to hit back the other person's bowling ball. It is no easier for me to "just listen" during a conversation, than it is for my Japanese students to "just relax" when speaking with foreigners. Now I can truly sympathize with how hard they must find it to try to carry on a western-style conversation.

If I have not yet learned to do conversational bowling in Japanese, at least I have figured out one thing that puzzled me for a long time. After his first trip to America, my husband complained that Americans asked him so many questions and made him talk so much at the dinner table that he never had a chance to eat. When I asked him why he couldn't talk and eat at the same time, he said that Japanese do not customarily think that dinner, especially on fairly formal occasions, is a suitable time for extended conversation.

Since westerners think that conversation is an indispensable part of dining, and indeed would consider it impolite not to converse with one's dinner partner, I found this Japanese custom rather strange. Still, I could accept it as a cultural difference even though I didn't really understand it. But when my husband added, in explanation, that Japanese consider it extremely rude to talk with one's mouth full, I got confused. Talking with one's mouth full is certainly not an American custom. We think it very rude, too. Yet we still manage to talk a lot and eat at the same time. How do we do it?

For a long time, I couldn't explain it, and it bothered me. But after I discovered the conversational ballgames, I finally found the answer. Of course! In a western-style conversation, you hit the ball, and while someone else is hitting it back, you take a bite, chew, and swallow. Then you hit the ball again, and then eat some more. The more people there are in the conversation, the more chances you have to eat. But even with only two of you talking, you still have plenty of chances to eat.

Maybe that's why polite conversation at the dinner table has never been a traditional part of Japanese etiquette. Your turn to talk would last so long without interruption that you'd never get a chance to eat.

QUESTIONS FOR DISCUSSION

1. What are the characteristics of a Japanese-style conversation? A Western-style conversation?
2. What analogies does the author use to describe each conversation style?

3. What can we infer about the different cultures based on the conversation styles?

QUESTIONS FOR WRITING

1. Compare/contrast the conversation styles of two other groups: men and women, friends vs. parents, etc.
2. Do you think Sakamoto provides an accurate description of Americans' conversation style? Why or why not?

"Education"

E. B. White

I have an increasing admiration for the teacher in the country school where we have a third-grade scholar in attendance. She not only undertakes to instruct her charges in all the subjects of the first three grades, but she manages to function quietly and effectively as a guardian of their health, their clothes, their habits, their mothers, and their snowball engagements. She has been doing this sort of Augean task for twenty years, and is both kind and wise. She cooks for the children on the stove that heats the room and she can cool their passions or warm their soup with equal competence. She conceives their costumes, cleans up their messes, and shares their confidences. My boy already regards his teacher as his great friend, and I think tells her a great deal more than he tells us.

The shift from city school to country school was something we worried about quietly all last summer. I have always rather favored public school over private school, if only because in public school you meet a greater variety of children. This bias of mine, I suspect, is partly an attempt to justify my own past (I never knew anything but public schools) and partly an involuntary defense against getting kicked in the shins by a young ceramist on his way to the kiln. My wife was unacquainted with public schools, never having been exposed (in her early life) to anything more public than the washroom of Miss Winsor's. Regardless of our backgrounds, we both knew that the change in schools was something that concerned not us but the scholar himself. We hoped it would work out all right. In New York our son went to a medium-priced private institution with semi-progressive ideas of education, and modern plumbing. He learned fast, kept well, and we were satisfied. It was an electric, colorful, regimented existence with moments of pleasurable pause and giddy incident. The day the Christmas angel fainted and had to be carried out by one of the Wise Men was educational in the highest sense of the term. Our scholar gave imitations of it around the house for weeks afterward, and I doubt if it ever goes completely out of his mind.

His days were rich in formal experience. Wearing overalls and an old sweater (the accepted uniform of the private seminary), he sallied forth at morn accompanied by a nurse or a parent and walked (or was pulled) two blocks to a corner where the school bus made a flag stop. This flashy vehicle was as punctual as death: seeing us waiting at the cold curb, it would sweep to a halt, open its mouth, suck the boy in, and spring away with an angry growl. It was a good deal like a train picking up a bag of mail. At school the scholar was worked on for six or seven hours by half a dozen teachers and a nurse, and was revived on orange juice in mid-morning. In a cinder court he played games supervised by an athletic instructor, and in a cafeteria he ate lunch worked out by a dietician. He soon learned to read with gratifying facility and discernment and to make Indian weapons of a semi-deadly nature. Whenever one of his classmates fell low of a fever the news was put on the wires and there were breathless phone calls to physicians, discussing periods of incubation and allied magic.

In the country all one can say is that the situation is different, and somehow more casual. Dressed in corduroys, sweatshirt, and short rubber boots, and carrying a tin dinner-pail, our scholar departs at crack of dawn for the village school, two and a half miles down the road, next to the cemetery. When the road is open and the car will start, he makes the journey by motor, courtesy of his old man. When the snow is deep or the motor is dead or both, he makes it on the hoof. In the afternoons he walks or hitches all or part of the way home in fair weather, gets transported in foul. The schoolhouse is a two-room frame building, bungalow type, shingles stained a burnt brown with weather-resistant stain. It has a chemical toilet in the basement and two teachers above stairs. One takes the first three grades, the other the fourth, fifth, and sixth. They have little or no time for individual instruction, and no time at all for the esoteric. They teach what they know themselves, just as fast and as hard as they can manage. The pupils sit still at their desks in class, and do their milling around outdoors during recess.

There is no supervised play. They play cops and robbers (only they call it "Jail") and throw things at one another—snowballs in winter, rose hips in fall. It seems to satisfy them. They also construct darts, pinwheels, and "pick-up sticks" (jackstraws), and the school itself does a brisk trade in penny candy, which is for sale right in the classroom and which contains "surprises." The most highly prized surprise is a fake cigarette, made of cardboard, fiendishly lifelike.

The memory of how apprehensive we were at the beginning is still strong. The boy was nervous about the change too. The tension, on that first fair morning in September when we drove him to school, almost blew the windows out of the sedan. And when later we picked him up on the road, wandering along with his little blue lunch-pail, and got his laconic report "All right" in answer to our inquiry about how the day had gone, our relief was vast. Now, after almost a year of it, the only difference we can discover in the two school experiences is that in the country he sleeps better at night—and *that* probably is more the air than the education. When grilled on the subject of school-in-country *vs.* school-in-city, he replied that the chief difference is that the day seems to go so much quicker in the country. "Just like lightning," he reported.

QUESTIONS FOR DISCUSSION

1. Which school does White prefer? Explain.
2. White uses only one example of a country school and one example of a city school, hardly enough to argue that EITHER city schools or country schools are better. What then is really being compared/contrasted in this essay?
3. Look closely at paragraph 3 where White describes the school bus. How does White use language to persuade the reader that one school is better than the other?

QUESTIONS FOR WRITING

1. White's essay was written 60 years ago. Is it still an accurate depiction of the difference in schools?
2. Compare/contrast two schools you have attended and argue why one is/was better than the other.

A Tale of Two Schools

Jonathan Kozol

New Trier's[1] physical setting might well make the students of Du Sable High School[2] envious. The *Washington Post* describes a neighborhood of "circular driveways, chirping birds and white-columned homes." It is, says a student, "a maple land of beauty and civility." While Du Sable is sited on one crowded city block, New Trier students have the use of 27 acres. While Du Sable's science students have to settle for makeshift equipment, New Trier's students have superior labs and up-to-date technology. One wing of the school, a physical education center that includes three separate gyms, also contains a fencing room, a wrestling room and studios for dance instruction. In all, the school has seven gyms as well as an Olympic pool.

The youngsters, according to a profile of the school in *Town and Country* magazine, "make good use of the huge, well-equipped building, which is immaculately maintained by a custodial staff of 48."

It is impossible to read this without thinking of a school like Goudy,[3] where there are no science labs, no music or art classes and no playground—and where the two bathrooms, lacking toilet paper, fill the building with their stench.

"This is a school with a lot of choices," says one student at New Trier; and this hardly seems an overstatement if one studies the curriculum. Courses in music, art and drama are so varied and abundant that students can virtually major in these subjects in addition to their academic programs. The modern and classical language department offers Latin (four years) and six other foreign languages. Elective courses include the literature of Nobel winners, aeronautics, criminal justice, and computer languages. In a senior literature class, students are reading Nietzsche, Darwin, Plato, Freud and Goethe. The school also operates a television station with a broadcast license from the FCC, which broadcasts on four channels to three counties.

Average class size is 24 children; classes for slower learners hold 15. This may be compared to Goudy—where a remedial class holds 39 children and a "gifted" class has 36.

[1]Suburban Chicago high school.—Ed.
[2]Inner-city Chicago school.—Ed.
[3]Inner-city Chicago school.—Ed.

Every freshman at New Trier is assigned a faculty adviser who remains assigned to him or her through graduation. Each of the faculty advisers—they are given a reduced class schedule to allow them time for this—gives counseling to about two dozen children. At Du Sable, where the lack of staff prohibits such reduction in class schedules, each of the guidance counselors advises 420 children.

The ambience among the students at New Trier, of whom only 1.3 percent are black, says *Town and Country*, is "wholesome and refreshing, a sort of throwback to the Fifties." It is, we are told, "a preppy kind of place." In a cheerful photo of the faculty and students, one cannot discern a single nonwhite face.

New Trier's "temperate climate" is "aided by the homogeneity of its students," *Town and Country* notes. ". . . Almost all are of European extraction and harbor similar values."

"Eighty to 90 percent of the kids here," says a counselor, "are good, healthy, red-blooded Americans."

The wealth of New Trier's geographical district provides $340,000 worth of taxable property for each child; Chicago's property wealth affords only one-fifth this much. Nonetheless, *Town and Country* gives New Trier's parents credit for a "willingness to pay enough . . . in taxes" to make this one of the state's best-funded schools. New Trier, according to the magazine, is "a striking example of what is possible when citizens want to achieve the best for their children." Families move here "seeking the best," and their children "make good use" of what they're given. Both statements may be true, but giving people lavish praise for spending what they have strikes one as disingenuous. "A supportive attitude on the part of the families in the district translates into a willingness to pay . . . ," the writer says. By this logic, one would be obliged to say that "unsupportive attitudes" on the part of . . . the parents of Du Sable's children translate into fiscal selfishness, when, in fact, the economic options open to the parents in these districts are not even faintly comparable. *Town and Country* flatters the privileged for having privilege but terms it aspiration.

"Competition is the lifeblood of New Trier," *Town and Country* writes. But there is one kind of competition that these children will not need to face. They will not compete against the children who attended . . . Du Sable. They will compete against each other and against the graduates of other schools attended by rich children. They will not compete against the poor. . . .

Conditions at Du Sable High School, which I visited in 1990, seem in certain ways to be improved. Improvement, however, is a relative term. Du Sable is better than it was three or four years ago. It is still a school that would be shunned—or, probably, shut down—if it were serving a white middle-class community. The building, a three-story Tudor structure, is in fairly good repair and, in this respect, contrasts with its immediate surroundings, which are almost indescribably despairing. The school, whose student population is 100 percent black, has no campus and no schoolyard, but there is at least a full-sized playing field and track. Overcrowding is not a problem at the school. Much to the reverse, it is uncomfortably empty. Built in 1935 and holding some 4,500 students in past years, its student population is now less than 1,600. Of these students, according to data provided by the school, 646 are "chronic truants."

The graduation rate is 25 percent. Of those who get to senior year, only 17 percent are in a college-preparation program. Twenty percent are in the general curriculum, while a stunning 63 percent are in vocational classes, which most often rule out college education.

A vivid sense of loss is felt by standing in the cafeteria in early spring when students file in to choose their courses for the following year. "These are the ninth graders," says a supervising teacher; but, of the official freshman class of some 600 children, only 350 fill the room. An hour later the eleventh graders come to choose their classes: I count at most 170 students.

The faculty includes some excellent teachers, but there are others, says the principal, who don't belong in education. "I can't do anything with them but I'm not allowed to fire them," he says, as we head up the stairs to visit classes on a day in early June. Entering a biology class, we find a teacher doing absolutely nothing. She tells us that "some of the students have a meeting," but this doesn't satisfy the principal, who leaves the room irate. In a room he calls "the math headquarters," we come upon two teachers watching a soap opera on TV. In a mathematics learning center, seven kids are gazing out the window while the teacher is preoccupied with something at her desk. The principal again appears disheartened.

Top salary in the school, he says, is $40,000. "My faculty is aging. Average age is 47. Competing against the suburbs, where the salaries go up to $60,000, it is very, very hard to keep young teachers. That, you probably know, is an old story. . . . I do insist," he says, "that every student has a book." He says this with some pride and, in the context of Chicago, he has reason to be proud of this; but, in a wealthy nation like America, it is a sad thing to be proud of.

In a twelfth grade English class, the students are learning to pronounce a list of words. The words are not derived from any context; they are simply written on a list. A tall boy struggles hard to read "fastidious," "gregarious," "auspicious," "fatuous." Another reads "dour," "demise," "salubrious," "egregious" and "consommé." Still another reads "aesthetic," "schism," "heinous," "fetish," and "concerto." There is something poignant, and embarrassing, about the effort that these barely literate kids put into handling these odd, pretentious words. When the tall boy struggles to pronounce "egregious," I ask him if he knows its meaning. It turns out that he has no idea. The teacher never asks the children to define the words or use them in a sentence. The lesson baffles me. It may be that these are words that will appear on one of those required tests that states impose now in the name of "raising standards," but it all seems dreamlike and surreal.

After lunch I talk with a group of students who are hoping to go on to college but do not seem sure of what they'll need to do to make this possible. Only one out of five seniors in the group has filed an application, and it is already April. Pamela, the one who did apply, however, tells me she neglected to submit her grades and college-entrance test results and therefore has to start again. The courses she is taking seem to rule out application to a four-year college. She tells me she is taking Spanish, literature, physical education, Afro-American history and a class she terms "job strategy." When I ask her what this is, she says, "It teaches how to dress and be on time and figure your deductions." She's a bright, articulate student, and it seems quite sad that she has not had any of the richness of curriculum that would have been given to her at a high school like New Trier.

The children in the group seem not just lacking in important, useful information that would help them to achieve their dreams, but, in a far more drastic sense, cut off and disconnected from the outside world. In talking of some recent news events, they speak of Moscow and Berlin, but all but Pamela are unaware that Moscow is the capital of the Soviet Union or that Berlin is in Germany. Several believe that Jesse Jackson is the mayor of New York City. Listening to their guesses and observing their confusion, I am thinking of the students at New Trier High. These children live in truly separate worlds. What do they have in common? And yet the kids before me seem so innocent and spiritually clean and also—most of all—so vulnerable. It's as if they have been stripped of all the armament—the words, the reference points, the facts, the reasoning, the elemental weapons—that suburban children take for granted. . . .

"It took an extraordinary combination of greed, racism, political cowardice and public apathy," writes James D. Squires, the former editor of the *Chicago Tribune*, "to let the public schools in Chicago get so bad." He speaks of the schools as a costly result of "the political orphaning of the urban poor . . . daytime warehouses for inferior students . . . a bottomless pit."

The results of these conditions are observed in thousands of low-income children in Chicago who are virtually disjoined from the entire world view, even from the basic reference points, of the American experience. A 16-year-old girl who has dropped out of school discusses her economic prospects with a TV interviewer.

"How much money would you like to make in a year?" asks the reporter.

"About $2,000," she replies.

The reporter looks bewildered by this answer. This teen-age girl, he says, "has no clue that $2,000 a year isn't enough to survive anywhere in America, not even in her world."

QUESTIONS FOR DISCUSSION

1. Find the points of comparison Kozol uses in this essay and discuss the details for each of the schools (i.e. physical facilities, etc.)
2. What does Kozol mean when he says that New Trier students "will not compete against the poor"?
3. What specifically is being compared/contrasted in this essay?

QUESTIONS FOR WRITING

1. Compare/contrast your own high school with those described in this essay.
2. Are the schools presented in this essay typical of good and bad schools? Why or why not? Use evidence from Kozol's essay as well as from your own experiences and observations.

Personal Worth

E. J. Dionne, Jr.

Which would you prefer kids to learn: **self-respect or self-esteem?**

I'd make a case that this is not an interesting question only about words but also about philosophy—and perhaps even psychology. The evidence is that self-esteem now far outstrips self-respect in the public discourse—by a huge margin, if my Internet and newspaper searches are any indication. But is self-esteem's apparent victory over self-respect in the conceptual wars a good thing? I'd claim that it's not, though I'd welcome arguments to the contrary.

The word "esteem" does have a noble sound to it, and in the dictionaries, its meaning overlaps with that of the word "respect." The *New College Edition of the American Heritage Dictionary*, for instance, defines esteem as "to regard as of a high order; think of with respect; prize." Respect, in turn, is defined as "to feel or show esteem for; to honor."

But Ronald Thiemann, dean of Harvard University's Divinity School, notes that the ancient meanings of the two words suggest a difference in emphasis.

In the old "cultures of honor," he said, esteem usually attached to rank. "The king deserved esteem no matter what he did," Dr. Thiemann said. The implication for self-esteem is that "I deserve esteem no matter what I do." Respect on the other hand, was earned by behaving in a certain way, and, he argues, also by accepting limits on one's behavior. Nobody out there needs to be convinced of how big the idea of self-esteem has become. But if you surf the Net, you might be astonished nonetheless at the range of books, activities and organizations that promise to help you raise your self-esteem—or somebody else's.

This being America, there's a National Association for Self-Esteem whose purpose is "to fully integrate self-esteem into the fabric of American society so that every individual, no matter what their age or background, experiences personal worth and happiness." There's the Self-Esteem Shop Online (*www.selfesteemshop.com*), which offers titles such as *Parents as Therapeutic Partners, 101 Ways to Be a Special Mom and Cutting Loose: Why Women Who End Their Marriages Do So Well.*

Self-esteem has entered the vocabulary in part as a response by members of groups that have suffered oppression or discrimination to what they see as society's effort to keep them down, and diminish their sense of self-worth. To the extent that the self-esteem movement is about the insistence that all human beings are worthy of respect—from themselves and others—the movement can be seen as a positive force.

My crankiness on the relative merit of self-respect over self-esteem is rooted in something else—the arrogance that can go along with too much self-esteem. As Martha Minow, a Harvard law professor and author of *Not Only for Myself*, explains it, the first definition of esteem "is about ranking, and if you add the 'self' to esteem, it's how you rank yourself." High self-esteem, in other words, can mean ranking yourself above everybody else. That breeds arrogance. Respect, on the other hand, carries a notion of dignity in relationship to others. Can you ever have too much self-respect?

Elisabeth Lasch-Quinn, a historian at Syracuse University, points to another aspect of self-esteem—it reflects the triumph of our therapeutic era.

Therapy is aimed at making people "feel good, feel comfortable." That's why you want self-esteem. "But the drive for self-respect is completely opposite in every way," she says. "It means being uncomfortable because you're in struggle, trying to live up to a standard of excellence or remaining true to your most deeply held moral beliefs."

Following from this, there is a vigorous debate among educators over whether teaching self-esteem helps kids learn by making them believe they can and are personally worthy or whether, on the contrary, the process of learning, performing tasks well and treating others decently must come prior to self-esteem (or, as I'd prefer, self-respect).

Lasch-Quinn suggests that if you want to trace the trajectory of ideas in American education, you could contrast the 19th century's emphasis on "character building" with the late-20th-century focus on self-esteem.

Minow's interest in this subject was inspired by the much-cited thought of the first-century sage Hillel: "If I am not for myself, who will be? If I am only for myself, who am I? If not now, when?" Of course we should have respect and, if you must, some esteem for ourselves. But in my gut, I fear that if we spend a few more decades promoting self-esteem, we might convince ourselves to forget that there's anyone of value out there—other than ourselves. "We can't have respect for ourselves if we're only for ourselves," Minow says. "We become egotistical selfish beasts." To feel that way would lower our self-esteem—and our self-respect, too.

QUESTIONS FOR DISCUSSION

1. According to the author, what is the difference between self-respect and self-esteem?
2. What does the author think is wrong with over-emphasis on self-esteem?
3. Why, according to the author, is self-respect more important than self-esteem?

QUESTIONS FOR WRITING

1. Which do you think is more important, self-respect, or self-esteem? Explain your answer. In supporting your points, you should refer to the article as well as to your own observations and experiences.
2. Choose two other concepts that may be confused and compare/contrast them to explain their different meanings.

"Lavender Twilight, Fairy Tale Blue Sparkling, Dazzling, Enchanted You . . ."

Ashley O'Kane

Student Essay

"Glazed, Amazed, and Color Dazed." "Lippity Slick." What's THAT about? "Soft shimmering shades that put stars in your eyes and lipsticks that dance 'til dawn." "Surrender to the Shine . . . because you're worth it." "Get a stick without the ick. New clean makeup sheer stick." The high gloss mega-impact pages of most women's magazines are ablaze with the lingo. But, as all socially refined, literate women of the civilized world will happily inform you, all makeup is not created equal. For the sake of discussion, there are two types of makeup: the kind you pick up at the grocery store with your quart of milk, and the kind you spend hours rapturously sampling and invest half of your paycheck on at an obscenely priced department store. Which, if given the option, would most women prefer? Or, perhaps more importantly, which SHOULD most women buy? It depends on a few different factors.

Comparatively, both types of makeup are equally useful because after all, some makeup is better than no makeup at all. Right? The goal is to hide that blotchy redness, that pimple so huge that it could be mistaken for a weather satellite pulsating in the middle of your forehead, the dark circles under your eyes—all the while enhancing the wearer's "natural" beauty. With this goal in mind, we can safely say that grocery store and department store brands both get the job done. In addition, both lines are available in self-contained attractive packing with equal ease of carrying in a makeup bag, purse, backpack, or jeans pocket. Containers are similarly so sturdy they can be carelessly dropped to the unyielding surface of a parking lot and still survive. Both types of makeup come complete with puffs, wands, applicators, brushes, and other accessories necessary for their proper use. It should be noted, however, that department store brands have additional utensils available, such as lash separators, brow brushes, and multi-use brushes in various sizes.

But consider this scenario. The biggest party of the social season started, without you, over an hour ago. In the heated rush to create the perfect "look" for the perfect night, you note your big brand name department store mascara tube is dry and empty. In a vain attempt to try and make your lashes reach their full potential—by adding normal tap water to the mascara container—you realize the situation is hopeless. Where can you buy mascara at 11 P.M. at night? Availability of grocery store makeup over department store makeup is a consideration. Certainly all the lab coat wearing sales girls at the Clinique counter at Macy's and Nordstrom's were in bed hours ago—or else they are at the biggest party of the social season. Steve, however, is ready and able to ring up your emergent purchase of Mabelline High Intensity Waterproof Mascara (available in sable brown AND midnight black conveniently located between the batteries and the dental floss) at the local AM/PM mini mart or Raley's Superstore. In a makeup emergency, grocery store brands win for convenience and availability.

For most women, though, personal attention is everything, especially when we are spending our hard earned cash. Department store makeup counters are all about personal attention. Attractive, but not too attractive—who wants to feel intimidated while confessing their beauty flaws such as oily areas and acne—well informed salespersons, fashionably dressed and naturally sporting the products they represent, personally see to it that colors, fragrances, and makeup types match the purchaser's skin type, complexion, lip shape, and hair highlights. This is a very scientific process that can take hours. It is an *experience*. In the local market, searching for an eye shadow to match that melon sequined evening dress, there is absolutely no personal consultation or assistance available. An inexperienced shopper can make terrible mistakes. Makeup is a non-returnable item, so you want to get it right the first tine. For personal attention and perfect accuracy, department store makeup is the way to go.

Being *chic* is important. There is nothing *chic* about grocery store makeup. You simply are the proud owner of a container of goo labeled "generic." No flashing lights, no "oohs" and "aahs," just get-the-job-done generic. This does not make a woman feel extra special or empowered. In contrast, however, when a pack of women go to the ladies room to reapply, friends and mere bystanders for that matter, will gasp when you produce a shiny chic monogrammed container etched *Lancome*. This will spark important social conversation, perhaps help influence that important business decision, or make a new friend. *Chic* is definitely important.

Let's talk money. Consumers are driven by value and cost. Department store makeup, compared to grocery store makeup, is pricey. A compact of Clinique pressed powder found at a department store specialty counter is about $17.00 while a compact of Covergirl powder available at any major grocery store is about $9.00. This is quite a difference. Two for one. But consider this. The Clinique compact is a one time cost of $17.00, and future refills are available for a mere five additional dollars. Covergirl does not offer a similar easy, breezy deal. In addition, one must consider the ever popular "free gift." If the Clinique compact is purchased during the free gift promotional time, it comes with a very chic makeup bag containing a gold mine full of delightful additional items. These range from purse size perfumes, mascara—a \$12 value—a full sized lipstick, moisturizer, hair products, eye shadow, AND foundation. Now that's a deal! Covergirl, or any other grocery store brand cannot compare. One additional item here is important. Clinique, as well as many other department store featured makeup brand—run the free gift promotions at different major stores at different times. If you stay alert to these promotions, you can frequent different stores, picking up free gifts to keep your makeup bag well supplied. Although the department store makeup may appear pricier, an alert, well informed, makeup consumer can clean up at the department store counter.

When considering grocery store and department store makeup brands, although generally overpriced and somewhat inconvenient, overall department store brands would get the vote of most discerning women. These brands offer variety, the opportunity to experiment with color, and the opportunity to be a bit self-indulgent. Moreover, the mere experience of spending the afternoon lounging at the makeup counter with girlfriends—and getting all those free gifts—are reasons enough to spend a little more money. After all, "you're worth it."

CHAPTER 7
Definition

EXTENDED DEFINITION: DEFINING IDEAS AND CONCEPTS

When you want to find the meaning of a particular word, the first place you look is probably your dictionary. The dictionary is often very useful in defining simple objects or concepts (i.e. "book," "desk," "sun," "school"), but when the word being defined is more abstract and/or complex (i.e. "love," "success," "beauty," "art") a more detailed, thorough definition may be needed. In defining these more complex ideas and concepts, *extended definition* can be a useful tool. Extended definition is a method of defining a term using a variety of strategies (discussed below) to illustrate and analyze it. The extended definition goes far beyond the dictionary's definition to provide a more in-depth, comprehensive definition. The following tips should prove useful as you write your extended definition essay.

Extended Definition can be used to define

- **Abstract ideas or concepts:** These are ideas or concepts that are not tangible; that is, they are not objects or beings that can be seen, heard, touched, etc. For example, **emotions,** such as *love, jealousy, pride,* and *happiness,* and **ideas** such as *justice, success, truth,* and *friendship* are all abstract.

- **Ambiguous terms or concepts:** These are terms or concepts whose meanings are not fixed; that is, they may be open to many different interpretations depending upon the perspective of the person defining them. A term or concept might also be ambiguous because it has changed in meaning over time or currently has multiple accepted meanings. Some examples of ambiguous terms or concepts are *harassment, prejudice, intelligence,* and *beauty.* **Note: Most ambiguous terms/concepts are also abstract.**

- **Controversial terms or concepts:** These are terms or concepts whose definitions are subject to controversy or debate. Often, the validity or credibility of a particular argument (in a court case, for example) rests almost entirely upon definitions of key terms. Controversial terms or concepts are those such as *sexual harassment, obscenity, free speech,* and *child abuse.* **Note: Many controversial** terms/concepts also fall into the "abstract" and "ambiguous" categories as well; the fact that they are abstract and/or ambiguous often leads to disagreements and controversy over their meanings.

Extended Definition Strategies

The secret to writing an effective extended definition essay is to use a variety of techniques to present a comprehensive, detailed definition that your reader will understand and accept. The best extended definition essays employ a combination of MOST of the following strategies:

- **Dictionary Definitions:** When starting work on your extended definition essay, the dictionary is often a good place to begin. You may use the dictionary's definition of a term or terms as a sort of "jumping off point" for your essay; this may involve presenting the definition and expanding on it, discussing its inadequacy, or even disagreeing with it. Your essay may require the use of dictionary definitions of two or more terms. For example, if your essay is on the subject of "child abuse" you might want to distinguish between "child abuse" and "discipline" (See E. J. Dionne's "Personal Worth" for an example of the use of dictionary definitions).

- **Examples:** As discussed in the "Exemplification" chapter of this book, examples are an effective strategy for supporting a thesis because they allow a reader to "see" an illustration of the ideas and concepts being presented. Whether they are real-life examples (from the news, your own experiences and observations, etc.) or *hypothetical* examples (examples you have created to illustrate a particular point), examples can help to make abstract ideas more concrete for your reader (see Robert Keith Miller's "Discrimination is a Virtue" as a model of how to use examples).

- **Negation:** One of the best ways to define a term or concept is to present what it is NOT. Negation is the strategy of defining a term or concept by defining its opposite and contrasting the two definitions. For example, if you are defining "success," you might also define "failure" and show how these two concepts are opposites. Similarly, if you want to define what true love is, you might contrast it with "attraction" and/or "infatuation." In using negation, you will most likely want to include the dictionary definitions of both terms as well as examples to illustrate both. In "How to Breed Intolerance," Sara Ziegler makes a distinction between "intolerance" and "disagreement."

- **Re-consideration:** Often, the writer of an extended definition essay will ask the reader to accept a definition of a term or concept that is very different from the commonly accepted one. Many words have two different levels of meaning: ***denotation*** (the literal meaning of the word, usually the dictionary definition) and ***connotation*** (the meaning of the word as determined by the emotions and/or judgments it evokes in the reader); many words have more than one connotation, but most have one particular connotation that is recognized by most people. The connotations of some words—and, at times, even the denotations—change over time, and a word which meant one thing 100 years ago may have an entirely different meaning (or several different meanings) today. Robert Keith Miller's "Discrimination is a Virtue" provides a good example of re-consideration, as Miller presents the difference between the original denotative meaning of "discrimination" and its current connotative meaning (prejudice).

Some Things to Remember When Writing an **Extended Definition:**

- **Choose a topic that is worthy of development.** Remember that tangible objects (book, computer, shoe) do not make good subjects of extended definition essays because they cannot be defined beyond their obvious denotative meanings (dictionary definitions). As discussed above, abstract, ambiguous, and controversial terms make the best topics for extended definition essays because the meanings of these terms are often vague and therefore open to interpretation and/or debate.

- **Provide a thesis that is clear, well-stated, and worthy of development.** Remember that a solid essay depends upon a well-crafted thesis. Review the section on thesis statements from Chapter 1.

- **Avoid simply narrating (telling a story).** Although some of the support for your extended definition essay will be provided in the form of examples, resist the urge to simply tell a story. Remember that the extended definition essay is an *analytical* essay that requires you to use a variety of techniques to achieve your purpose.

- **Stick to ONE main term or concept.** The purpose of the extended definition essay is to provide the reader with YOUR definition of a particular term or concept. While some topics may require brief definitions of several terms, your essay should be focused primarily on ONE term or concept. Attempting to focus on a number of different terms may result in confusion for both you and your reader as your essay will lack focus.

On Friendship

Margaret Mead and Rhoda Metraux

Few Americans stay put for a lifetime. We move from town to city to suburb, from high school to college in a different state, from a job in one region to a better job elsewhere, from the home where we raise our children to the home where we plan to live in retirement. With each move we are forever making new friends, who become part of our new life at that time.

For many of us the summer is a special time for forming new friendships. Today millions of Americans vacation abroad, and they go not only to see new sights but also—in those places where they do not feel too strange—with the hope of meeting new people. No one really expects a vacation trip to produce a close friend. But surely the beginning of a friendship is possible? Surely in every country people value friendship?

They do. The difficulty when strangers from two countries meet is not a lack of appreciation of friendship, but different expectations about what constitutes friendship and how it comes into being. In those European countries that Americans are most likely to visit, friendship is quite sharply distinguished from other, more casual relations, and is differently related to family life. For a Frenchman, a German or an Englishman friendship is usually more particularized and carries a heavier burden of commitment.

But as we use the word, "friend" can be applied to a wide range of relationships—to someone one has known for a few weeks in a new place, to a close business associate, to a childhood playmate, to a man or woman, to a trusted confidant. There are real differences among these relations for Americans—a friendship may be superficial, casual, situational or deep and enduring. But to a European, who sees only our surface behavior, the differences are not clear.

As they see it, people known and accepted temporarily, casually, flow in and out of Americans' homes with little ceremony and often with little personal commitment. They may be parents of the children's friends, house guests of neighbors, members of a committee, business associates from another town or even another country. Coming as a guest into an American home, the European visitor finds no visible landmarks. The atmosphere is relaxed. Most people, old and young, are called by first names.

Who, then, is a friend?

Even simple translation from one language to another is difficult. "You see," a Frenchman explains, "if I were to say to you in France, 'This is my good friend,' that person would not be as close to me as someone about whom I said only, 'This is my friend.' Anyone about whom I have to say *more* is really less."

In France, as in many European countries, friends generally are of the same sex, and friendship is seen as basically a relationship between men. Frenchwomen laugh at the idea that "women can't be friends," but they also admit sometimes that for women "it's a different thing." And many French people doubt the possibility of a friendship between a man and a woman. There is also the kind of relationship within a group—men and women who have worked together for a long time, who may be very close, sharing great loyalty and warmth of feeling. They may call one another *copains*—a word that in English becomes "friends" but has more the feeling of "pals" or "buddies." In French eyes this is not friendship, although two members of such a group may well be friends.

For the French, friendship is a one-to-one relationship that demands a keen awareness of the other person's intellect, temperament and particular interests. A friend is someone who draws out your own best qualities, with whom you sparkle and become more of whatever the friendship draws upon. Your political philosophy assumes more depth, appreciation of a play becomes sharper, taste in food or wine is accentuated, enjoyment of a sport is intensified.

And French friendships are compartmentalized. A man may play chess with a friend for thirty years without knowing his political opinion, or he may talk politics with him for as long a time without knowing about his personal life. Different friends fill different niches in each person's life. These friendships are not made part of family life. A friend is not expected to spend evenings being nice to children or courteous to a deaf grandmother. These duties, also serious and enjoined, are primarily for relatives. Men who are friends may meet in a café. Intellectual friends may meet in larger groups for evenings of conversation. Working people may meet in the little *bistro* where they drink and talk, far from the family. Marriage does not affect such friendships; wives do not have to be taken into account.

In the past in France, friendships of this kind seldom were open to any but intellectual women. Since most women's lives centered on their homes, their warmest relations with other women often went back to their girlhood. The special relationship of friendship is based on what the French value most—on the mind, on compatibility of outlook, on vivid awareness of some chosen area of life.

Friendship heightens the sense of each person's individuality. Other relationships commanding as great loyalty and devotion have a different meaning. In World War II the first resistance groups formed in Paris were built on the foundation of *les copains*. But significantly, as time went on these little groups, whose lives rested in one another's hands, called themselves "families." Where each had a total responsibility for all, it was kinship ties that provided the model. And even today such ties, crossing every line of class and personal interest, remain binding on the survivors of these small, secret bands.

In Germany, in contrast with France, friendship is much more articulately a matter of feeling. Adolescents, boys and girls, form deeply sentimental attachments, walk and talk together—not so much to polish their wits as to share their hopes and fears and dreams, to form a common front against the world of schools and family and to join in a kind of mutual discovery of each other's and their own inner life. Within the family, the closest relationship over a lifetime is between brothers and sisters. Outside the family, men and women find in their closest friends of the same sex the devotion of a sister, the loyalty of a brother. Appropriately, in Germany friends usually are brought into the family. Children call their father's and their mother's friends "uncle" and "aunt." Between French friends, who have chosen each other for the congeniality of their point of view, lively disagreement and sharpness of argument are the breath of life. But for Germans, whose friendships are based on mutuality of feeling, deep disagreement on any subject that matters to both is regarded as a tragedy. Like ties of kinship, ties of friendship are meant to be irrevocably binding. Young Germans who come to the United States have a great difficulty in establishing such friendships with Americans. We view friendship more tentatively, subject to changes in intensity as people move, change their jobs, marry, or discover new interests.

English friendships follow still a different pattern. Their basis is shared activity. Activities at different stages of life may be of very different kinds—discovering a common interest in school, serving together in the armed forces, taking part in a foreign mission, staying in the same country house during a crisis. In the midst of the activity, whatever it may be, people fall into step—sometimes two men or two women, sometimes two couples, sometimes three people—and find that they walk or play a game or tell stories or serve on a tiresome and exacting committee with the same easy anticipation of what each will do day by day or in some critical situation. Americans who have made English friends comment that, even years later, "you can take up just where you left off." Meeting after a long interval, friends are like a couple who begin to dance again when the orchestra strikes up after a pause. English friendships are formed outside the family circle, but they are not, as in Germany, contrapuntal to the family nor are they, as in France, separated from the family. And a break in an English friendship comes not necessarily as a result of some irreconcilable difference of viewpoint or feeling but instead as a result of misjudgment, where one friend seriously misjudges how the other will think or feel or act, so that suddenly they are out of step.

What, then, is friendship? Looking at these different styles, including our own, each of which is related to a whole way of life, are there common elements? There is the recognition that friendship, in contrast with kinship, invokes freedom of choice. A friend is someone who chooses and is chosen. Related to this is the sense each friend gives the other of being a special individual, on whatever grounds this recognition is based. And between friends there is inevitably a kind of equality of give and take.

These similarities make the bridge between societies possible, and the American's characteristic openness to different styles of relationships makes it possible for him to find new friends abroad with whom he feels at home.

QUESTIONS FOR DISCUSSION

1. How do friendships in different European countries differ from one another? How do they differ from American friendships?
2. What are some common characteristics that are shared by friendships in countries all around the world?
3. Do the authors provide a concrete definition of friendship? If so, what is it?

QUESTIONS FOR WRITING

1. Based on what you have read in the article and on your own experiences living in America, provide a definition of "friendship" from an American perspective. Use examples from the article to compare and contrast your definition of friendship with the ones provided by the authors.
2. Look up the dictionary definition of "friend" and discuss how the various types of friendships described in the article do (or do not) coincide with the dictionary's definition (you might want to look up the definition of "friend" in a dictionary in another language as well).

Discrimination Is a Virtue

Robert Keith Miller

When I was a child, my grandmother used to tell me a story about a king who had three daughters and decided to test their love. He asked each of them "How much do you love me?" The first replied that she loved him as much as all the diamonds and pearls in the world. The second said that she loved him more than life itself. The third replied "I love you as fresh meat loves salt."

This answer enraged the king; he was convinced that his youngest daughter was making fun of him. So he banished her from his realm and left all of his property to her elder sisters.

As the story unfolded it became clear, even to a 6-year-old, that the king had made a terrible mistake. The two older girls were hypocrites, and as soon as they had profited from their father's generosity, they began to treat him very badly. A wiser man would have realized that the youngest daughter was the truest. Without attempting to flatter, she had said, in effect, "We go together naturally; we are a perfect team."

Years later, when I came to read Shakespeare, I realized that my grandmother's story was loosely based upon the story of King Lear, who put his daughters to a similar test and did not know how to judge the results. Attempting to save the king from the consequences of his foolishness, a loyal friend pleads, "Come sir, arise, away! I'll teach you differences." Unfortunately, the lesson comes too late. Because Lear could not tell the difference between true love and false, he loses his kingdom and eventually his life.

We have a word in English which means "the ability to tell differences." That word is *discrimination*. But within the last twenty years, this word has been so frequently misused that an entire generation has grown up believing that "discrimination" means "racism." People are always proclaiming that "discrimination" is something that should be done away with. Should that ever happen, it would prove to be our undoing.

Discrimination means discernment; it means the ability to perceive the truth, to use good judgment and to profit accordingly. The *Oxford English Dictionary* traces this understanding of the word back to 1648 and demonstrates that, for the next 300 years, "discrimination" was a virtue, not a vice. Thus, when a character in a nineteenth-century novel makes a happy marriage, Dickens has another character remark, "It does credit to your discrimination that you should have found such a very excellent young woman."

Of course, "the ability to tell differences" assumes that differences exist, and this is unsettling for a culture obsessed with the notion of equality. The contemporary belief that discrimination is a vice stems from the compound "discriminate against." What we need to remember, however, is that some things deserve to be judged harshly: we should not leave our kingdoms to the selfish and the wicked.

Discrimination is wrong only when someone or something is discriminated against because of prejudice. But to use the word in this sense, as so many people do, is to destroy its true meaning. If you discriminate against something because of general preconceptions rather than particular insights, then you are not discriminating—bias has clouded the clarity of vision which discrimination demands.

One of the great ironies of American life is that we manage to discriminate in the practical decisions of daily life, but usually fail to discriminate when we make public policies. Most people are very discriminating when it comes to buying a car, for example, because they realize that cars have differences. Similarly, an increasing number of people have learned to discriminate in what they eat. Some foods are better than others—and indiscriminate eating can undermine one's health.

Yet in public affairs, good judgment is depressingly rare. In many areas which involve the common good, we see a failure to tell differences.

Consider, for example, some of the thinking behind modern education. On the one hand, there is a refreshing realization that there are differences among children, and some children—be they gifted or handicapped—require special education. On the other hand, we are politically unable to accept the consequences of this perception. The trend in recent years has been to group together students of radically different ability. We call this process "mainstreaming," and it strikes me as a characteristically American response to the discovery of differences: we try to pretend that differences do not matter.

Similarly, we try to pretend that there is little difference between the sane and the insane. A fashionable line of argument has it that "everybody is a little mad" and that few mental patients deserve long-term hospitalization. As a consequence of such reasoning, thousands of seriously ill men and women have been evicted from their hospital beds and returned to what is euphemistically called "the community"—which often means being left to sleep on city streets, where confused and helpless people now live out of paper bags as the direct result of our refusal to discriminate.

Or to choose a final example from a different area: how many recent elections reflect thoughtful consideration of the genuine differences among candidates? Benumbed by television commercials that market aspiring officeholders as if they were a new brand of toothpaste or hair spray, too many Americans vote with only a fuzzy understanding of the issues in question. Like Lear, we seem too eager to leave the responsibility of government to others and too ready to trust those who tell us whatever we want to hear.

So as we look around us, we should recognize that "discrimination" is a virtue which we desperately need. We must try to avoid making unfair and arbitrary distinctions, but we must not go to the other extreme and pretend that there are no distinctions to be made. The ability to make intelligent judgments is essential both for the success of one's personal life and for the functioning of society as a whole. Let us be open-minded by all means, but not so open-minded that our brains fall out.

QUESTIONS FOR DISCUSSION

1. In what way(s) is discrimination a "virtue"?
2. What distinctions does the author make between "discrimination" and the two terms it is commonly confused with, "racism" and "prejudice"?
3. What does Miller mean in the final sentence when he says, "Let us be open-minded by all means, but not so open-minded that our brains fall out"?

QUESTIONS FOR WRITING

1. Analyze Miller's use of the extended definition techniques described at the beginning of this chapter. How does he use these techniques in presenting his definition of discrimination?
2. In paragraph 5, Miller writes, "People are always proclaiming that discrimination is something that should be done away with. Should that ever happen, it would prove to be our undoing." Do you agree or disagree? Explain your answer, using points from Miller's article and your own ideas and observations.

Bully, Bully

John Leo

DO GOSSIP AND RUMORS COUNT AS PUNISHABLE BEHAVIOR?

Now we have a big national study on bullying, and the problem with it is right there in the first paragraph: Bullying behavior may be "verbal (e.g., name-calling, threats), physical (e.g., hitting), or psychological (e.g., rumors, shunning/exclusion)." Uh-oh. The study may or may not have put bullying on the map as a major national issue. But it rather clearly used a dubious tactic: taking a lot of harmless and minor things ordinary children do and turning them into examples of bullying. Calling somebody a jerk and spreading rumors counted as bullying in the study. Repeated teasing counted too. You achieved bully status if you didn't let the class creep into your game of catch, or if you just stayed away from people you didn't like (shunning, exclusion).

With a definition like that, the total of children involved in either bullying or being bullied themselves ought to be around 100 percent. But no, the bullying study says only 29.9 percent of the students studied reported frequent or moderate involvement—and that total was arrived at by lumping bullies and their victims together in the statistics.

Debatable Definitions The low numbers and highly debatable definitions undercut the study's conclusion that bullying is "a serious problem for U.S. youth." Of the 29.9 figure, 13.0 percent were bullies, 10.6 percent were targets of bullying, and 6.3 percent were both perpetrators and victims. The study, done by the National Institute of Child Health and Human Development, is based on 15,686 questionnaires filled out by students in grades six through 10 in public and private schools around the country.

We have seen this statistical blending of serious and trivial incidents before. The American Association of University Women produced a 1993 report showing that 80 percent of American students have been sexually harassed, including a hard-to-believe 76 percent of all boys. The AAUW got the numbers up that high by including glances, gestures, gossip, and naughty jokes. The elastic definition encouraged schools and courts to view many previously uncontroversial kinds of expression as sexual harassment. Before long, schools were making solemn lists of harassing behaviors that included winking, and calling someone "honey."

Another set of broad definitions appeared when zero-tolerance policies descended on the schools. Antidrug rules were extended to cover aspirin. Antiweapons regulations covered a rubber knife used in a school play. Just two months ago, a third grader in Monroe, La., was suspended for drawing a picture of G.I. Joe. Now the antibullying movement is poised to provide a third source of dubious hyperregulation of the young. One antibullying specialist says "hard looks" and "stare downs"—everyday activities for millions of hormone-driven adolescents—should be punishable offenses under student codes.

This has all the makings of an antibullying crusade with many of the same wretched excesses of the zero-tolerance and anti-harassment campaigns. Serious bullying can be ugly. Parents and schools should stop it and punish offenders. And schools should do whatever they can to create a culture of civility and tolerance. But rumors and dirty looks and putting up with horrible classmates are a part of growing up. So are the teenage tendencies to form cliques and snub people now and then. Adults shouldn't faint when they see this behavior, or try to turn it into quasi-criminal activity.

Another pitfall: In focusing on gossip, rumors, and verbal offenses, the crusade has the obvious potential to infringe on free speech at schools. Will comments like "I think Catholicism is wrong," or "I think homosexuality is a sin," be turned into antibullying offenses? The crusade could also demonize those who bully, instead of helping them change. Some of the antibully literature circulating in Europe is hateful stuff. One screed calls "the serial bully" glib, shallow, evasive, incapable of intimacy, and a practiced liar who "displays a seemingly limitless demonic energy." Yet a lot of the academic literature reports that bullies often aren't very psychologically different from their victims. And the national study says a fifth of bullying victims are bullies themselves.

The example of Europe's more advanced antibullying crusade should make Americans cautious. The European campaign has expanded from schools into the adult world and the workplace. Several nations are considering antibullying laws, including Britain. Definitions are expanding too. A proposed antibullying law in Portugal would make it illegal to harass workers by giving them tasks for which they are overqualified. Deliberately giving employees erroneous information would count as bullying too. Ireland's antibullying task force came up with a scarily vague definition of bullying: "repeated inappropriate behavior, direct or indirect," which could "reasonably be regarded as undermining the individual's right to dignity at work." Imagine what the American litigation industry could do with wording like that.

It's time to stop and ask: Where is our antibullying campaign going?

QUESTIONS FOR DISCUSSION

1. What are the behaviors that are a part of the "new" definition of bullying? Why does the author object to this current definition of bullying?

2. How are European countries dealing with the problem of bullying? What objections does the author have to these countries' anti-bullying methods?
3. Does the author believe that no anti-bullying measures should be taken at all?

QUESTIONS FOR WRITING

1. According to John Leo, "Rumors and dirty looks and putting up with horrible classmates are a part of growing up." What do you think? Explain your answer, using quotes and examples from the article and your own ideas, observations, and experiences.
2. What, in your opinion, constitutes bullying? Provide and explain your definition of "bullying." Be sure to use the extended definition techniques discussed at the beginning of this chapter.

Disarming the Rage

Richard Jerome, Ron Arias, Mary Boone, Lauren Comander,

Joanne Fowler, Maureen Marrington, Ellen Mazo, Jamie

Reno, Don Sider, Gail Cameron Wescott

Across the country, thousands of students stay home from school each day, terrified of humiliation or worse at the hands of bullies. In the wake of school shootings—most recently in California and Pennsylvania—parents, teachers and lawmakers are demanding quick action.

In the rigid social system of Bethel Regional High School in Bethel, a remote town in the tundra of southwest Alaska, Evan Ramsey was an outcast, a status earned by his slight frame, shy manner, poor grades and broken family. "Everybody had given me a nickname: Screech, the nerdy character on *Saved by the Bell*," he recalls. "I got stuff thrown at me, I got spit on, I got beat up. Sometimes I fought back, but I wasn't that good at fighting." Taunted throughout his years in school, he reported the incidents to his teachers, and at first his tormentors were punished. "After a while [the principal] told me to just start ignoring everybody. But then you can't take it anymore."

On the morning of Feb. 19, 1997, Ramsey, then 16, went to school with a 12-gauge shotgun, walked to a crowded common area and opened fire. As schoolmates fled screaming, he roamed the halls shooting randomly—mostly into the air. Ramsey would finally surrender to police, but not before killing basketball star Josh Palacios, 16, with a blast to the stomach, and principal Ron Edwards, 50, who was shot in the back. Tried as an adult for murder, Ramsey was sentenced to 210 years in prison after a jury rejected a defense contention that he had been attempting "suicide by cop," hoping to be gunned down but not intending to kill anyone. Still, Ramsey now admits in his cell at Spring Creek Correctional Center in Seward, Alaska, "I felt a sense of power with a gun. It was the only way to get rid of the anger."

Unfortunately Ramsey is not alone. Children all over the country are feeling fear, hopelessness and rage, emotions that turn some of them into bullies and others into their victims. Some say that is how it has always been and always will be—that bullying, like other adolescent ills, is something to be endured and to grow out of. But that view is changing. At a time when many parents are afraid to send their children to school, the wake-up call sounded by the 13 killings and 2 suicides at Columbine High School in Colorado two years ago still reverberates. It is now clear that

Columbine shooters Dylan Klebold and Eric Harris felt bullied and alienated, and in their minds it was payback time.

In recent months there have been two other horrifying shooting incidents resulting, at least in part, from bullying. On March 5, 15-year-old Charles "Andy" Williams brought a .22-cal. pistol to Santana High School in Santee, Calif., and shot 15 students and adults, killing 2. He was recently certified to stand trial for murder as an adult. His apparent motive? Lethal revenge for the torment he had known at the hands of local kids. "We abused him pretty much, I mean verbally," concedes one of them. "I called him a skinny faggot one time."

Two days after the Williams shooting, Elizabeth Bush, 14, an eighth grader from Williamsport, Pa., who said she was often called "idiot, stupid, fat, ugly," brought her father's .22-cal. pistol to school and shot 13-year-old Kimberly Marchese, wounding her in the shoulder. Kimberly, one of her few friends, had earned Elizabeth's ire by allegedly turning on her and joining in with the taunters. Bush admitted her guilt and offered apologies. A ward of the court until after she turns 21, she is now in a juvenile psychiatric facility. Kimberly, meanwhile, still has bullet fragments in her shoulder and is undergoing physical therapy.

As school enrollment rises and youths cope with the mounting pressures of today's competitive and status-conscious culture, the numbers of bullied children have grown as rapidly as the consequences. According to the National Education Association, 160,000 children skip school each day because of intimidation by their peers. The U.S. Department of Education reports that 77 percent of middle and high school students in small midwestern towns have been bullied. And a National Institutes of Health study newly released in the *Journal of the American Medical Association* reveals that almost a third of 6th to 10th graders—5.7 million children nationwide—have experienced some kind of bullying. "We are talking about a significant problem," says Deborah Prothrow-Stith, professor of public health practice at Harvard, who cites emotional alienation at home as another factor in creating bullies. "A lot of kids have grief, loss, pain, and it's unresolved."

Some experts see bullying as an inevitable consequence of a culture that rewards perceived strength and dominance. "The concept of power we admire is power over someone else," says Jackson Katz, 41, whose Long Beach, Calif., consulting firm counsels schools and the military on violence prevention. "In corporate culture, in sports culture, in the media, we honor those who win at all costs. The bully is a kind of hero in our society." Perhaps not surprisingly, most bullies are male. "Our culture defines masculinity as connected to power, control and dominance," notes Katz, whose work was inspired in part by the shame he felt in high school when he once stood idly by while a bully beat up a smaller student.

As for the targets of bullying, alienation runs like a stitch through most of their lives. A study last fall by the U.S. Secret Service found that in two-thirds of the 37 school shootings since 1974, the attackers felt "persecuted, bullied, threatened, attacked or injured." In more than three-quarters of the cases, the attacker told a peer of his violent intentions. William Pollack, a clinical psychologist and author of *Real Boys' Voices*, who contributed to the Secret Service study, said that several boys from Columbine described bullying as part of the school fabric. Two admitted to mocking Klebold and Harris. "Why don't people get it that it drives you over the edge?" they told Pollack. "It isn't just Columbine. It is everywhere."

That sad fact is beginning to sink in, as the spate of disturbing incidents in recent years has set off desperate searches for answers. In response, parents have begun crusades to warn and educate other families, courts have seen drawn-out legal battles that try to determine who is ultimately responsible, and lawmakers in several states—including Texas, New York and Massachusetts—have struggled to shape anti-bullying legislation that would offer remedies ranging from early intervention and counseling to the automatic expulsion of offenders.

One of the most shocking cases of victimization by bullies took place near Atlanta on March 28, 1994. That day, 15-year-old Brian Head, a heavyset sophomore at suburban Etowah High School, walked into economics class, pulled out his father's 9-mm handgun and pressed it to his temple. "I can't take this anymore," he said. Then he squeezed the trigger. Brian had been teased for years about his weight. "A lot of times the more popular or athletic kids would make him a target," his mother, Rita, 43, says of her only child, a sensitive boy with a gift for poetry. "They would slap Brian in the back of the head or push him into a locker. It just broke him." Not a single student was disciplined in connection with his death. After his suicide, Rita, a magazine copy editor, and her husband, Bill, 47, counseled other parents and produced a video for elementary school students titled *But Names Will Never Hurt Me* about an overweight girl who suffers relentless teasing.

Georgia residents were stunned by a second child's death on Nov. 2, 1998. After stepping off a school bus, 13-year-old Josh Belluardo was fatally punched by his neighbor Jonathan Miller, 15, who had been suspended in the past for bullying and other infractions. In that tragedy's wake Georgia Gov. Roy Barnes in 1999 signed an anti-bullying law that allows schools to expel any student three times disciplined for picking on others.

On the other side of the continent, Washington Gov. Gary Locke is pressing for anti-bullying training in schools, following two high-profile cases there. Jenny Wieland of Seattle still cannot talk of her only child, Amy Ragan, shot dead at age 17 more than eight years ago, without tearing up. A soccer player and equestrian in her senior year at Marysville-Pilchuck High School, Amy was heading to the mall on the night of Nov. 20, 1992, when she stopped at a friend's apartment. There, three schoolmates had gathered by the time Trevor Oscar Turner showed up. Then 19, Turner was showing off a .38-cal. revolver, holding it to kids' heads, and when he got to Amy, the weapon went off. Turner pleaded guilty to first-degree manslaughter and served 27 months of a 41-month sentence.

"I can't help but wonder what Amy's life would be like if she was still alive," says Wieland today. "I wonder about her career and if she'd be in love or have a baby." Wieland turned her grief into action. In 1994 she helped start Mothers Against Violence in America (MAVIA), an activist group patterned after Mothers Against Drunk Driving. She left her insurance job to become the program's director and speaks annually at 50 schools. In 1998 she became the first director of SAVE (Students Against Violence Everywhere), which continues to grow, now boasting 126 student chapters nationwide that offer schools anti-harassment and conflict-resolution programs. "People ask how I can stand to tell her story over and over," she says. "If I can save just one child, it's well worth the pain."

Not long after Amy Ragan's death, another bullying scenario unfolded 50 miles away in Stanwood, Wash. Confined to a wheelchair by cerebral palsy, Calcutta-born Taya Haugstad was a fifth grader in 1993, when a boy began calling her "bitch" and "retard." The daily verbal abuse led to terrible nightmares. By middle school, according to a lawsuit Taya later filed, her tormentor—a popular athlete—got physical, pushing her wheelchair into the wall and holding it while his friends kicked the wheels. Eventually Taya was diagnosed with posttraumatic stress disorder. "Imagine that you can't run away or scream," says her psychologist, Judith McCarthy. "Not only was she traumatized, she's handicapped. She felt terribly unsafe in the world." Her adoptive parents, Karrie and Ken Haugstad, 48 and 55, complained to school authorities and went to court to get a restraining order against the bully, but it was never issued. Taya sued the school district and the boy in 1999. The judge awarded her $300,000 last year, ruling that the school was negligent in its supervision, thus inflicting emotional distress. (The ruling is under appeal.) Taya, now 19 and a high school junior, hopes to study writing in college. She says she holds no grudge against her nemesis, who received undisclosed punishment from the school. "I don't think about him," she says.

But Josh Sneed may never forgive the boys he refers to as the Skaters. It was in 1996, late in his freshman year at Powell High School in Powell, Tenn., when, he says, a group of skateboarders began to terrorize him. With chains clinking and baseball bats pounding the pavement, he claims, they chased him and threatened to beat him to death. Why Josh? He was small and "a country boy," says his homemaker mother, Karen Grady, 41. "They made fun of him for that. They told him he was poor and made fun of him for that."

Then on Oct. 17, 1996, "I just snapped," her son says. As Jason Pratt, known as one of the Skaters, passed him in the cafeteria, Sneed whacked him on the head with a tray. "I figured if I got lucky and took him out, all the other nonsense would stop." But after a few punches, Josh slipped on a scrap of food, hit his head on the floor and lost consciousness as Pratt kneed him in the head several times. Finally a football player leapt over two tables and dragged Sneed away, likely saving his life. Four titanium plates were needed to secure his shattered skull, and he was so gravely injured that he had to relearn how to walk and talk. Home-schooled, Sneed eventually earned his GED, but he hasn't regained his short-term memory. Assault charges against both him and Pratt were dismissed, but Pratt (who declined to comment) was suspended from school for 133 days.

Grady sued the county, claiming that because the school knew Josh was being terrorized but never disciplined the tormentors, they effectively sanctioned the conditions that led to the fight. Her attorney, James A. H. Bell, hopes the suit will have national implications. "We tried to make a statement, holding the school system accountable for its failure to protect," he says. In February Sneed and Grady were awarded $49,807 by a judge who found the county partly at fault. A tractor buff who once aspired to own a John Deere shop, Josh now lives on his grandfather's farm, passing his days with cartoons, video games and light chores. "Everybody's hollering that they need to get rid of guns, but it's not that," he says. "You need to find out what's going on in school."

Around the country, officials are attempting to do precisely that, as many states now require a safe-school plan that specifically addresses bullying. Most experts agree that metal detectors and zero-tolerance expulsions ignore the root of the problem. Counseling and fostering teamwork seem most effective, as evidenced by successful programs in the Cherry Creek, Colo., school district and DeKalb Country, Ga. "We create an atmosphere of caring—it's harder to be a bully when you care about someone," says John Monferdini, head counselor at the DeKalb Alternative School, which serves 400 county students, most of whom have been expelled for bullying and violent behavior. Apart from academics, the school offers conflict-resolution courses and team-oriented outdoor activities that demand cooperation, "Yeah, I'm a bully," says Chris Jones, 15. "If I'm with friends and we see someone coming along we can jump on, we do it. It's like, you know, an adrenaline rush." But a stint in DeKalb is having a transformative effect. "When I came here, it was because we beat up a kid so badly—sticking his head in the bleachers—and the only thing I wished was that we'd had a chance to hurt him worse before we got caught. That's not the way I am now."

One wonders if intervention might have restrained the bullies who tormented Evan Ramsey. Ineligible for parole until 2066, when he'll be 86, Ramsey, now 20, spends most days working out, playing cards, reading Stephen King novels and studying for his high school diploma. He also has plenty of time to reflect on the horrible error in judgment he made. "The worst thing is to resort to violence," he says. "I'd like to get letters from kids who are getting problems like I went through. I could write back and help them." His advice: "If they're being messed with, they have to tell someone. If nothing's done, then they have to go [to] higher and higher [authority] until it stops. If they don't get help, that's when they'll lose it and maybe do something bad—really bad. And the pain of doing that never really stops."

QUESTIONS FOR DISCUSSION

1. What point are the authors making about bullying?
2. What are some of the examples the authors use in the article? What purpose do these examples serve?
3. How do the authors define "bully," "bullying," and "victim"?

QUESTIONS FOR WRITING

1. The authors quote Jackson Katz, whose consulting firm counsels schools and the military on violence and who says that "the bully is a kind of hero in our society." Do you think this is true? Respond to Katz's point, using points from the article and your own ideas, observations, and experiences.
2. According to the article, attitudes toward bullying have become more serious in recent years, and many schools in particular are taking steps to curtail bullying. What do you think should be done to eliminate (or at least decrease) bullying in our society? Explain your answer, using points from the article and your own ideas, observations, and experiences.

How to Breed Intolerance

Sara Ziegler

Know as little as possible. Rely on rumor and speculation. Ignore facts. Utilize stereotypes. Spread your views to others in the hopes that they, too, will learn to hate. This is how you breed intolerance.

Intolerance is the art of ignoring any views that differ from your own. It manifests itself in hatred, discrimination, prejudice, and stereotypes. Once it festers in people, intolerance is nearly impossible to overcome. But why would anyone want to be labeled *intolerant*? Why would people want to be uninformed about the world around them? Why would one want to be part of the problem in America, instead of the solution?

There are many explanations for intolerant attitudes, some dating back to childhood. It is likely that intolerant folks grew up imitating intolerant parents and the cycle of prejudice has simply continued for generations. Perhaps intolerant people are so set in their ways that they find it easier to ignore anything that might not conform to their limited view of life. Or maybe intolerant students have simply never been exposed to anyone different from themselves. But none of these reasons is an excuse for allowing the intolerance to continue.

Intolerance should not be confused with disagreement. It is, of course, possible to disagree with an opinion without being intolerant of it. If you understand a belief but still don't believe in that specific belief, that's fine. You are entitled to your opinion. In fact, knowledgeable dissenters are important for any belief. If we all believed the same things, we would never grow, and we would never learn about the world around us. Intolerance does not stem from disagreement. It stems from fear. And fear stems from ignorance. When you are ignorant about homosexuality, you will distort the facts to fit your opinions. You will discount science and say things like, "Regardless of what geneticists and researchers may say when they try to link homosexuality in some way to a biological source. . . ." You will make up nonexistent "facts" about behaviors of homosexuals, insinuating they are all pedophiles. And you will belittle an entire category of people because, ultimately, your argument consists of nothing but an irrational fear of the unknown.

To tolerate a belief or stance does not mean you share these views. In fact, *Webster's New World Dictionary* defines the verb *tolerate* as "to respect others' beliefs, practices, etc. without sharing them." When "tolerating" others, you do disagree with them. But you disagree with them while respecting their right to their own opinion.

Intolerance isn't about your personal beliefs that are contrary to others'; it's about your actions toward them and your lack of respect for their views. It is entirely appropriate to disagree with a particular creed because of religious convictions. This is not necessarily "hiding behind the Bible." Once again, believing different creeds is not intolerance; not *respecting* different creeds is intolerance. And the Bible never justifies treating anyone differently based on what they believe.

Even though intolerance is frequently a set behavior, rooted deeply in many people's lives, there are ways to change opinions and actions. If you know and associate with homosexuals, you are infinitely more likely to be tolerant of them. You will learn, your prejudice will cease, and no one will need to erect a safe zone to protect homosexuals from you.

All you need to do to avoid intolerance is to respect each person for who they are—something everyone should be doing anyway.

QUESTIONS FOR DISCUSSION

1. What is the author's thesis?
2. What, according to the author, are the causes of intolerance?
3. How does "intolerance" differ from "disagreement"?

QUESTIONS FOR WRITING

1. Define one of the following terms: prejudice, racism, bias, or discrimination. Use the extended definition techniques presented at the beginning of this chapter.
2. According to Ziegler, "Intolerance does not stem from disagreement. It stems from fear. And fear stems from ignorance." What do you think? Discuss what you think are the causes of intolerance in our society. You may refer to the article, but you should also include discussion and analysis of your own ideas, experiences, and observations.

CHAPTER 8

Argument and Persuasion

ARGUMENTATION: MAKING AND SUPPORTING A CLAIM

Although you may not realize it, you have probably engaged in an argument almost every day since you learned to speak. Though the word "argument" usually brings to mind an image of two people angrily discussing a subject in loud voices, many arguments you will encounter or be a part of will involve no shouting at all. In fact, most arguments simply consist of one person (the arguer) making a statement to another person or persons (the audience) and then supporting that statement with evidence. Whether you are explaining to your parents why they should let you borrow their car or debating with your friends about who will win the baseball game over the weekend, argument probably plays a big role in your day to day life. Throughout your academic career, you will often be asked to write essays in which you make and support an argument. This chapter will explain how to present a good argument to your audience.

An argument is made up of two essential parts

- **The CLAIM** is the overall point you want to make. It answers the question "What are you trying to prove?" Since the claim is also your thesis, it should be worthy of development and should be clearly and assertively stated (see Chapter 1 for review of the thesis). Keep in mind that the claim MUST be something debatable that can be supported.

The following are examples of ineffective claims:

- I think public school students shouldn't be made to wear uniforms.
- Should college teachers be permitted to grade on attendance?
- Kids behave really badly in schools today.

These claims are much more effective:

- Requiring public school students to wear uniforms infringes on the students' rights.

- Attendance should not be a factor in college students' end-of-semester course grades.
- It is the responsibility of both schools and parents to educate children in the proper ways to behave and treat others.

- **The EVIDENCE** is the material used to support your claim. Evidence can be in the form of **facts, statistics, examples, and definitions:**

Facts/Statistics:

Mary Pipher talks about the "selves" of girls going down in flames. One effect of a crashing self is suicide. *Six times* as many boys as girls commit suicide. In 1992, fully 4,044 young males (ages 15 to 24) killed themselves. Among same-age females there were 649 suicides. To the extent that there is a gender gap among youth, it is boys who turn out to be on the fragile side.

(From "The 'Fragile American Girl' Myth" by Christina Hoff Sommers)

Examples:

. . . in public affairs, good judgment is depressingly rare. In many areas which involve the common good, we see a failure to tell differences.

Consider, for example, some of the thinking behind modern education. On the one hand, there is a refreshing realization that there are differences among children, and some children – be they gifted or handicapped – require special education. On the other hand, we are politically unable to accept the consequences of this perception. This trend in recent years has been to group together students of radically different ability. We call this process "mainstreaming," and it strikes me as a characteristically American response to the discovery of differences: we try to pretend that differences do not matter.

(From "Discrimination is a Virtue" by Robert Keith Miller)

Definition:

To tolerate a belief or stance does not mean you share these views. In fact, *Webster's New World Dictionary* defines the verb *tolerate* as "to respect others' beliefs, practices, etc. without sharing them." When "tolerating" others, you do disagree with them. But you disagree with them while respecting their right to their own opinion.

(From "How to Breed Intolerance" by Sara Ziegler)

Do's and Don'ts of Argumentation

DO . . .

- Make a claim that is debatable, relevant, interesting, and that can be supported with a sufficient amount of evidence.
- Use an assertive tone that helps to establish your authority as a writer. If it is clear that YOU believe your claim, your reader is more likely to be interested in what you have to say.

- Provide evidence that clearly and effectively supports your claim.
- Acknowledge the opposing side of the argument to assure your reader that you are ***knowledgeable*** (that you are aware of all sides of the issue) and ***credible*** (that you are believable and trustworthy).

DON'T . . .

- Make a claim on a topic you don't feel strongly about. If you don't care about the topic, it will show; your argument will be lacking, and your reader will not be interested to read what you have to say.
- Make a claim on a topic that is obvious or one that is not really debatable. For example, "Child abuse is wrong" is not a debatable claim because few—if any—would argue that child abuse is acceptable, so there is really nothing to prove.
- Support your claim solely with your opinions, experiences, and emotions. Remember, your job as a writer is to provide strong, relevant support to prove your claim. Though arguing certainly involves giving your opinion, an argument based almost entirely on expression of your emotions about the topic or on your personal experiences will lack the credibility of an argument supported with concrete evidence.

Exercise: Argument Practice

Choose one of the following and construct a brief (approx 1-2 page) argument using the guidelines provided in this chapter:

1. Write a letter to the president or top administrator of your college in which you argue in favor of making a change in some college policy, procedure, or situation that you feel is unfair, unnecessary, or detrimental to students (for example, the college's lack of night and weekend classes, the operating hours of the library, cafeteria or another service on campus, the parking situation, etc.). Remember to keep your audience in mind and use the appropriate tone and level of formality.
2. Write an editorial in which you present and argue in favor of a plan to improve the city/community in which you live. Write your argument as if you were writing for your local newspaper.
3. Choose a controversial issue that is currently in the news and write an argument in which you support your stance on the issue. Be sure to include information about the issue to familiarize your audience with it.

The 'Fragile American Girl' Myth

Christina Hoff Sommers

Did you know that the United States Congress now categorizes American girls as "a historical underserved population"? In a recent education statute, girls are classified with African Americans, Native Americans, the physically handicapped, and other disadvantaged minorities as a group in need of special redress. Programs to help girls who have allegedly been silenced and demoralized in the nation's sexist classrooms are now receiving millions of federal dollars. At the United Nations Women's Conference in Beijing, the alleged silencing and short-changing of American schoolgirls was treated as a pressing human rights issue.

Several popular books have appeared in recent years to build up the notion that ours is a "girl-poisoning culture." That phrase is Dr. Mary Piper's, and her book, *Reviving Ophelia: Saving the Selves of Adolescent Girls*, has been at the top of the *New York Times* bestseller list. According to Piper, "Something dramatic happens to girls in early adolescence. Just as planes and ships disappear mysteriously into the Bermuda Triangle, so do the selves of girls go down in droves. They crash and burn."

Where did she get this idea? Where did the United States Congress get the idea that girls are a victim group? How did the "silencing" of American schoolgirls become an international human rights issue?

To answer that, consider some highlights of what might be called the myth of the incredible shrinking girl. The story epitomizes what is wrong with the contemporary women's movement. First, a few facts.

The U.S. Department of Education keeps records of male and female school achievement. They reveal that girls get better grades than boys. Boys are held back more often than girls. Significantly fewer boys than girls go on to college today. Girls are a few points behind in national tests of math and science, but that gap is closing. Meanwhile, boys are *dramatically* behind in reading and writing. We never hear about that gap, which is not shrinking.

Many more boys than girls suffer from learning disabilities. In 1990, three times as many boys as girls were enrolled in special education programs. Of the 1.3 million American children taking Ritalin, the drug for hyperactivity, three-quarters are boys. More boys than girls are involved in crime, alcohol, drugs.

Mary Piper talks about the "selves" of girls going down in flames. One effect of a crashing self is suicide. *Six times* as many boys as girls commit suicide. In 1992, fully 4,044 young males (ages 15 to 24) killed themselves. Among same-age females there were 649 suicides. To the extent that there is a gender gap among youth, it is boys who turn out to be on the fragile side.

This is not to deny that some girls are in serious trouble, or that we can't do better by girls, educationally and otherwise. What I am saying is, you cannot find any responsible research that shows that girls, as a group, are worse off than boys, or that girls are an underprivileged class. So, where did that idea come from? Therein lies a tale.

The reality is, the contemporary women's movement is obsessed with proving that our system is rigged against women. No matter what record of success you show them, they can always come up with some example of oppression. Never is good news taken as real evidence that things have changed. The women's movement is still fixated on victimology. Where they can't prove discrimination, they invent it.

I, for one, do not believe American women are oppressed. It is simply irresponsible to argue that American women, as a gender, are worse off than American men.

More women than men now go to college. Women's life expectancy is seven years longer than men's. Many women now find they can choose between working full-time, part-time, flex-time, or staying home for a few years to raise their children. Men's choices are far more constricted. They can work full-time. They can work full-time. Or they can work full-time.

The reason we hear nothing about men being victims of society, or boys suffering unduly from educational and psychological deficits, is because the feminist establishment has the power to shape national discussion and determine national policy on gender issues.

Feminist research is advocacy research. When the American Association of University Women released a (badly distorted) survey in 1991 claiming that American girls suffer from a tragic lack of self-esteem, a *New York Times* reporter got AAUW President Sharon Shuster to admit that the organization commissioned the poll in order to get data into circulation that would support its officers' belief that schoolgirls were being short-changed. Usually, of course, belief comes after, not before, data-gathering. But advocacy research doesn't work that way. With advocacy research, first you believe, and then you gather figures you can use to convince people you are right.

The myth of the short-changed schoolgirl is a perfect example of everything that's gone wrong with contemporary feminism. It's all there: the mendacious advocacy research, the mean-spiritedness to men that extends even to little boys, the irresponsible victimology, the outcry against being "oppressed," coupled with massive lobbying for government action.

The truth is, American women are the freest in the world. Anyone who doesn't see this simply lacks common sense.

QUESTIONS FOR DISCUSSION

1. What is Sommers' claim?
2. What kinds of evidence does Sommers use in supporting her claim?
3. What, according to Sommers, are the causes of the "fragile American girl myth"?

QUESTIONS FOR WRITING

1. Who is better off in today's American society, males or females? Discuss which gender faces more difficulties/obstacles in America today. Be sure to support your answer with facts, examples, and other types of evidence discussed in this chapter.
2. At the end of the essay, Sommers argues that "American women are the freest in the world. Anyone who doesn't see this simply lacks common sense." Do you agree with this statement? Support your answer, using the various types of support discussed in this chapter.

From *The American Enterprise, May-June 1997, V. 8, N. 3* by Christina H. Sommers.

Bigger

Jim Sollisch

Every day, you read how the world is becoming a smaller place. Every article that talks about the growing number of households on the Internet mentions that the world is shrinking, as if every new AOL subscriber diminishes the earth's mass just a little more. In fact, if you read the business pages of any paper, you know we don't even live in a *"world"* anymore—we live in a global community. We are fellow travelers in a global age. We communicate globally. Our markets are global. Our capabilities are global. Our vision is global. With all this global intimacy, it's no wonder my kids think the world is roughly the size of Rhode Island. After all, they can hop on the Internet and be chatting with someone in Australia in seconds.

But that just means the world is moving faster and faster, not growing smaller. How did we get the two confused? Just because I can order a book from Amazon.com in nineteen seconds doesn't mean the world has become a cozy little hamlet. In the real world—as opposed to the digital world—small usually means slower, not faster.

For example, there's a little used bookstore in my neighborhood. It carries one-thousandth of the books Amazon.com carries and yet, choosing one takes a hundred times longer. And that's the good news. You wander around in a completely nonlinear way. You pick up a book on motorcycle maintenance. Next to that is a Jane Austen novel. You're looking it over to try to figure out if they've turned this one into a movie yet when your eye catches an old Spiderman comic book. The bookstore works like your mind—free association run amok. At Amazon.com, linear logic is the order of the day. Author, title, subject, ca-ching, thank you very much.

If speed means smallness, then fast food places would be called "small food" places because they can sure move you out quick. Big-Mac, fries, supersize it, have a nice day. But go to a really small restaurant run by people who actually prepare your food rather than push it along a conveyor belt, and you'll be there a while. Enjoy the atmosphere. Relax. If you're lucky, your food will take a long time to prepare. The longer, the better.

When you're in a restaurant like that, then the world really is a smaller place. Same with the local hardware store. It's a lot smaller than Home Depot or Lowe's. And you may have to wait for the owner to finish explaining to Mr. Johnson how to apply dope to the PVC joint, but it's worth the wait because he'll be happy to show you how to rewire the lamp you brought in. And if you need one extra screw, he'll probably give it to you. Whereas at Home Depot you'll have to buy a box of 500. And since Home Depots are opening at every intersection in America, it seems to me that the world is getting bigger by a factor of 500 or so.

I hate bigness, especially when it masquerades as smallness. I'm sick of stores the size of GM plants that sell everything from cereal bowls to satellite dishes. I'm sick of people telling me how wonderful it is that I can buy an authentic dhurrie rug woven by villagers in Nepal over the Internet without leaving the comfort of my own home. I want to leave my home. I really do. I want to wander through tiny stores owned by the people who work the cash register. I want to be in my neighborhood, which really is a smaller place.

QUESTIONS FOR DISCUSSION

1. How does Sollisch differentiate between a "small" world and a "big" one?
2. What are the advantages of a smaller world, according to Sollisch?
3. What are the disadvantages of a bigger world?

QUESTIONS FOR WRITING

1. In your opinion, which is better, a "big" world or a "small" one? Support your claim using the types of evidence discussed in the chapter.
2. Sollisch argues against the notion that due to technology and corportate expansion the world is becoming a smaller place. What do you think? Support your answer with points from the article and the types of evidence discussed in this chapter.

Waste

Wendell Berry

As a country person, I often feel that I am on the bottom end of the waste problem. I live on the Kentucky River about ten miles from its entrance into the Ohio. The Kentucky, in many ways a lovely river, received an abundance of pollution from the Eastern Kentucky coal mines and the central Kentucky cities. When the river rises, it carries a continuous raft of cans, bottles, plastic jugs, chunks of Styrofoam, and other imperishable trash. After the floods subside, I, like many other farmers, must pick up the trash before I can use my bottomland fields. I have seen the Ohio, whose name (*Oho* in Iroquois) means "beautiful river," so choked with this manufactured filth that an ant could crawl dryfooted from Kentucky to Indiana. The air of both river valleys is seriously polluted. Our roadsides and roadside fields lie under a constant precipitation of cans, bottles, the plastic-ware of fast food joints, soiled plastic diapers, and sometimes whole bags of garbage. In our country we now have a "sanitary landfill" which daily receives, in addition to our local production, fifty to sixty large truckloads of garbage from Pennsylvania, New Jersey, and New York.

Moreover, a close inspection of our countryside would reveal, strewn over it from one end to the other, thousands of derelict and worthless automobiles, house trailers, refrigerators, stoves, freezers, washing machines, and dryers, as well as thousands of unregulated dumps in hollows and sink holes, on streambanks and roadsides, filled not only with "disposable" containers but also with broken toasters, television sets, toys of all kinds, furniture, lamps, stereos, radios, scales, coffee makers, mixers, blenders, corn poppers, hair dryers, and microwave ovens. Much of our waste problem is to be accounted for by the intentional flimsiness and un-repairability of the labor-savers and gadgets that we have become addicted to.

Of course, my sometime impression that I live on the receiving end of this problem is false, for country people contribute their full share. The truth is that we Americans, all of us, have become a kind of human trash, living our lives in the midst of a ubiquitous damned mess of which we are once the victims and the perpetrators. We are all unwilling victims, perhaps; and some of us even are unwilling perpetrators; but we must count ourselves among the guilty nonetheless. In my household we produce much of our own food and try to do without as many frivolous "necessities" as possible—and yet, like everyone else, we must shop, and when we shop we must bring home a load of plastic, aluminum, and glass containers designed to be thrown away, and "appliance" designed to wear out quickly and be thrown away.

I confess that I am angry at the manufacturers who make these things. There are days when I would be delighted if certain corporation executives could somehow be obliged to eat their products. I know of no good reason why these containers and all other forms of manufactured "waste"—solid, liquid, toxic, or whatever—should not be outlawed. There is no sense and no sanity in objecting to the desecration of the flag while tolerating and justifying and encouraging as a daily business the desecration of the country for which it stands.

But our waste problem is not the fault only of producers. It is the fault of an economy that is wasteful from top to bottom—a symbiosis of an unlimited greed at the top and a lazy, passive, and self-indulgent consumption at the bottom—and all of us are involved in it. If we wish to correct this economy, we must be careful to understand and to demonstrate how much waste of human life is involved in our waste of the material goods of creation. For example, much of the litter that now defaces our country is fairly directly caused by the massive secession of exclusion of most of our people from active participation in the food economy. We have made a social ideal of minimal involvement in the growing and cooking of food. This is one of the dearest "liberations" of our affluence. Nevertheless, the more dependent we become on the *industries* of eating and drinking, the more waste we are going to produce. The mess that surrounds us, then, must be understood not just as a problem in itself but as a symptom of a greater and graver problem: the centralization of our economy, the gathering of the productive property and power into fewer and fewer hands, and the consequent destruction, everywhere, of the local economies of household, neighborhood, and community.

This is the source of our unemployment problem, and I am not talking just about the unemployment of eligible members of the "labor force." I mean also the unemployment of children and old people, who, in viable household and local economies, would have work to do by which they would be useful to themselves and to others. The ecological damage of centralization and waste is thus inextricably involved with human damage. For we have, as a result, not only a desecrated, ugly, and dangerous country in which to live until we are in some manner poised by it, and a constant and now generally accepted problem of unemployed or unemployable workers, but also classrooms full of children who lack the experience and discipline of fundamental human tasks, and various institutions full of still capable old people who are useless and lonely.

I think that we must learn to see the trash on our streets and roadsides, in our rivers, and in our woods and fields, not as the side effects of "more jobs" as its manufacturers invariably insist that it is, but as evidence of good work *not* done by people able to do it.

QUESTIONS FOR DISCUSSION

1. What does Berry mean when he writes that our economy is "wasteful from top to bottom"?
2. What role does the "average" citizen have in creating the waste problem Berry writes about?
3. Do we indulge in too many "frivolous 'necessities' " as Berry writes? Which "wasteful" necessity could you not live without?

QUESTIONS FOR WRITING

1. Do you see the problem of waste described by Berry in the area where you live? If so, what do you think are the causes and/or the effects?
2. Berry writes that "much of the litter that now defaces our country is fairly directly caused by the massive secession of exclusion of most of our people from active participation in the food economy." Do you agree or disagree with this statement? Analyze some of Berry's examples as well as your own experiences and/or observations.

"Waste" from *What Are People For?* by Wendall Berry. Copyright © 1990 by Wendell Berry. Reprinted by permission of North Point Press, a division of Farrar, Straus and Giroux, LLC.

SUVs: Killer Cars

Ellen Goodman

For my second career, I want to write car ads. Or better yet, I want to live in a car ad.

In the real world, you and I creep and beep on some misnomered expressway, but in the commercial fantasy land, drivers cruise along deserted, tree-lined roads.

We stall and crawl on city streets, but the man in the Lexus races "in the fast lane"—on an elevated road that curves around skyscrapers. We circle the block, looking for a place to park, but the owner of a Toyota RAV4 pulls up onto the sandy beach. We get stuck in the tunnel, but the Escalade man navigates down empty streets because "there are no roadblocks."

The world of the car ads bears about as much resemblance to commuter life as the Marlboro ads bear to the cancer ward.

All of this is a prelude to a full-boil rant against the archenemy of commuters everywhere: sport utility vehicles. Yes, those gasguzzling, parking space-hogging bullies of the highway.

These sport utility vehicles are bought primarily by people whose favorite sport is shopping and whose most rugged athletic event is hauling the kids to soccer practice.

The sales and the size of the larger SUVs have grown at a speed that reminds me of the defense budget. In the escalating highway arms race, SUVs are sold for self-defense. Against what? Other SUVs.

As someone who has spent many a traffic-jammed day in the shadow of a behemoth, I am not surprised that the high and weighty are responsible for some 2,000 additional deaths a year. If a 6,000-pound Suburban hits an 1,800-pound Metro, it's going to be bad for the Metro. For that matter, if the Metro hits the Suburban, it's still going to be bad for the Metro.

The problem with SUVs is that you can't see over them, you can't see around them and you have to watch out for them. I am by no means the only driver of a small car who has felt intimidated by the big wheels barreling past me. Their macho reputation prompted even the Automobile Club of Southern California to issue an SUV driver tip: "Avoid a 'road warrior' mentality. Some SUV drivers operate under the false illusion that they can ignore common rules of caution."

But the biggest and burliest of the pack aren't just safety hazards; they're environmental hazards. Until now, SUVs have been allowed to legally pollute two or three times as much as automobiles. All over suburbia there are people who conscientiously drive their empty bottles to the suburban recycling center in vehicles that get 15 miles to the gallon.

There are parents putting big bucks down for a big car so the kids can be safe while the air they breathe is being polluted.

At long last some small controls are being promoted. The EPA has proposed for the first time that SUVs be treated like cars. If the agency, and the administration, has its way, a Suburban won't be allowed to emit more than a Taurus. That's an important beginning, but not the whole story.

Consider Ford, for example. The automaker produces relatively clean-burning engines. But this fall it will introduce the humongous Excursion. It's 7 feet tall, 80 inches wide, weighs 4 tons and gets 10 miles to the gallon in the city. No wonder the Sierra Club* calls it "the Ford Valdez†." This is a nice car for taking the kids to school—if you're afraid you'll run into a tank.

Do I sound hostile? Last week a would-be SUV owner complained to the *New York Times'* ethics critic that his friends were treating him as if he were "some kind of a criminal." The ethicist wrote back: "If you're planning to drive that SUV in New York, pack a suitcase into your roomy cargo area, because you're driving straight to hell."

I wouldn't go that far, though I have wished that hot trip on at least one SUV whose bumper came to eye level with my wind-shield. Still, the SUV backlash is growing so strong that today's status symbol may become the first socially unacceptable vehicle since cars lost their fins.

It's one thing to have an SUV in the outback and quite another to drive it around town. In the end, the right place for the big guy is in an ad. There, the skies are always clean, the drivers are always relaxed and there's never, ever another car in sight.

QUESTIONS FOR DISCUSSION

1. What is Goodman's opinion of SUVs?
2. What evidence does Goodman offer to support her claims about SUVs?
3. What does Goodman mean when she concludes that "in the end, the right place for the big guy [SUV] is in an ad"?

QUESTIONS FOR WRITING

1. In the essay, Goodman calls SUVs "gas-guzzling, parking space-hogging bullies of the highway . . . bought primarily by people whose favorite sport is shopping and whose most rugged athletic event is hauling kids to soccer practice." Do you agree with Goodman's arguments against SUVs? Support your answer using the types of evidence discussed in this chapter.
2. In the conclusion of the essay, Goodman argues that the "right place" for SUVs is "in an ad." What do you think? Support your answer using the types of evidence discussed in this chapter.

Guzzling, Gorgeous & Grand:
SUVs and Those Who Love Them

Dave Shiflett

Readers of Dickens[1] may occasionally imagine what it might have been like to peer from the guillotine and see Madame Defarge[2] knitting her Book of Sin. One would expect a look of terrifying certitude and ferocity, and while having one's head severed would constitute a profound setback on many fronts, one would at least be without her. As it happens, the old girl has many descendants in our own time, some of whom are glaring at me.

The indictment: Those of us who drive sport utility vehicles are guilty of crimes against fellow drivers, the environment, and world stability. We must be left horseless, if not headless.

This is a terrible turn of events. The fact is, we SUV drivers are peaceful, humble people of modest hopes and dreams, who happen to like driving around in large vehicles, often because they accommodate our heaving guts, which often reflect an infatuation with the handiwork of Harland Sanders[3] and August Busch.[4] Yet when we see ourselves denounced by our detractors, it is as if an alien race were being described.

We readily admit that our Big Rides use a bit more gas than the 48 horsepower vehicles (add 3hp when sails are raised) favored by those who would save the world from us. We are talking about the difference between the 27 miles per gallon average for regular automobiles and the 20 mpg rating of many SUVs. Because global warming is an article of faith among our critics, we're getting additional blame for melting icecaps, flooded coastlines, and the eventual appearance of palm trees in New York City.

We believe these charges are grossly exaggerated, and we also reject the assertion that our beloved tanks are killing machines. Official statistics tell us that around 4 percent of road fatalities are the result of SUV-auto crashes, which is of course terrible, but not all those accidents are our fault. Overall, SUVs are blamed for an additional 2,000 deaths per year, though as journalist Ken Smith has pointed out, that number is entirely speculative and must be taken very lightly.

---

[1]Charles Dickens was the English author of *A Tale of Two Cities*, a novel about the French Revolution, a triumph of the common people over the aristocrats.
[2]Madame Defarge is a character from Dickens' novel.
[3]Harland Sanders is the founder of Kentucky Fried Chicken.
[4]August Busch is the founder of a brewery.

Our critics are hardly inclined to do so. Sen. Dianne Feinstein, whose calmly sculptured coiffure cannot conceal what some call her Inner Inquisitor, calls us a subspecies of "energy gluttons" and backs legislation that would force us back into the slightly modified go-carts that pass for "mid-sized sedans." Ms. Geneva Overholser, whose placid first name cannot conceal a slightly hectoring personality, has denounced SUVs as "inexplicably popular extravagances" and "nonsensical, gas-guzzling behemoths." Geneva, who was once ombudsman for the *Washington Post*, even admitted that "I feel like a lunatic about SUVs, and I hereby invite you to join me in raving."

A line quickly formed. A. J. Nomai said the SUV "fad" is "all the rage among yuppies, suburban families and seemingly testosterone unbalanced males." Columnist Ellen Goodman called SUVs "gas-guzzling, parking space-hogging bullies of the highway." Bullying, as we have come to know, was the cause of the Columbine massacre, so this is a serious charge. Ms. Goodman also insists "the SUV backlash is growing so strong that today's status symbol may become the first socially unacceptable vehicle since cars lost their fins."

This all adds up to what crime specialists call a gang bang, and because we are suburban types who steer clear of that kind of activity, we're in shock. This is especially true when our kids join the fray. We understand, of course, that this kind of protest reflects our peaceful and prosperous times. The Cold War is over, and our youth, having had their molars sealed in infancy, have never even worried about tooth decay. As Bill Clinton (who goes around in very large vehicles) said after taking an egg in the ear, it's good for kids to be mad about something, and this is certainly a safe subject.

We can also chuckle over the fact that, for many of our critics, mass transit means taking an Airbus to Nice. We were especially gratified by recent news reports that DNC[5] chief Terry McAuliffe drives a Cadillac SUV that gets about 10 miles to the gallon, while Dick Gephardt,[6] currently on the warpath against "energy gluttons," drives a Ford SUV. These leaders, it was further reported, have garaged their Big Rides until the political assault on the president's energy policy is over.

Which, it seems, is what much of this criticism is about. We SUVers are mere pawns in a larger war. The people on the other side not only want us all to drive cars whose backseat passengers have to ride with their chins on their knees; they have a thing for windmills, solar panels, boarded-up nuclear-power plants, and kerosene lamps. They also tend to support mandatory-seatbelt laws, antismoking ordinances, and restrictions on home barbecuing. We understand that, in California, they went after weed whackers and leaf blowers—and won.

---

[5]The DNC is the Democratic National Committee.
[6]Dick Gephardt is a congressional leader of the Democratic Party.

Now it is SUV drivers who are in the crosshairs of the new Defarges, and we're being demonized as irrational and "unbalanced" beings, making it all the easier to whack us. Yet we're not nearly the menaces we're cracked up to be, as perhaps my own story illustrates.

My first SUV was a 1989 Ford Bronco II. This was no bully machine, but instead a pathetic vehicle whose first engine went out at 52,000 miles (Ms. Goodman tells us she drives a Saab, which, of course, is just perfect.) The Bronco passed into the nether world after a roll-over accident, which critics will find pleasing. That the 16-year-old driver was doing 45 down a 15-mile-per-hour stretch of Hairpin Alley, swerved into a steep ditch, and overcorrected, may have had something to do with the crash, though one hates to point fingers. In any event, the mangled Bronco was replaced by a Toyota 4-Runner, purchased with 138,000 miles on the odometer. The SUV community, as it happens, admires diverse peoples, the Japanese among them, especially since they build machines that last. This one should go 300,000 miles, and because of my relatively light driving schedule that means 20 years of service, by which time we may well have been forced into vehicles that pass muster with environmental activists, such as rickshaws. This is not a complaint. I have sent my wife into training in anticipation of this development, and should it arrive we will go quietly, save for the occasional crack of the accelerator.

Meanwhile, our aged 4-Runner performs its commonplace duties, such as hauling sound equipment for a variety of humble bands that entertain humble citizens at humble watering holes. It also provides a place to sleep during music festivals and road trips. Ms. Goodman, who no doubt snoozes in her Saab between speaking engagements, should be able to empathize. Indeed, if she would only reach out to SUV owners as she does to members of other victim classes, she might find we are merely her fellow men.

Doubtful. It sometimes seems that another major beef against the Big Ride is curiously sexual in nature. Ms. Goodman makes the point: "I am old enough to remember when the shape of a car was female, Detroit's sex appeal was all curves and cars were pitched to men with blondes draped over their hood. Now we're sold bivouac cars with brawn. It's no accident, one reader reminded me, that the Nissan Pathfinder was nicknamed the 'hardbody.' If the minivan is the soccer mom, the SUV is the muscle man, even when it's driven by a woman."

Taken together with the observation about "testosterone unbalanced males," we start to sense that our critics are not merely out to park vehicles. They believe they're shutting down the four-wheeled version of the stag room. Many of us do not understand how people got such an idea, though we are somewhat comforted in knowing that perhaps we're not the only loons in this dispute.

QUESTIONS FOR DISCUSSION

1. What is the purpose of Shiflett's argument?
2. What are the qualities that make smaller cars undesirable, according to Shiflett?
3. How does Shiflett respond to critics of SUVs?

QUESTIONS FOR WRITING

1. After reading both Shiflett's and Goodman's articles about SUVs, what is YOUR opinion of SUV's? Support your opinion, using points and examples from the readings and your own ideas, observations, and experiences.
2. Analyze both Shiflett's and Goodman's arguments in terms of the points they make, the evidence they use to support their points, and the tones they use. Which, in your opinion, makes a more valid argument? Support your answer with analysis of both of the articles as well as the types of evidence discussed in this chapter.

PART III

THE HANDBOOK

Previous sections of this book have discussed the following:

- The essay and its components
- How to write an essay
- Different methods for organizing material
- How to read critically—and effectively
- How to respond to reading and include the ideas of others in your writing

But you may be able to successfully master all of the above and still not produce an effective essay. Why? Because of your sentences. Why are sentences so important?

- What if you have won the lottery and you receive the following instructions?

  If you want to claim your $1,000,000 prize, bring slkuui within 24 hours.

  If you don't know what "slkuui" is, as I'm sure you don't, then you may never be able to collect your money.

- Or, imagine that you are leaving instructions for your teenage son:

  Take off your sneakers in the refrigerator. You will find some cookies.

  If your son only reads the first part of these instructions, you may end up with a very smelly refrigerator. What this writer probably means is **Take off your sneakers. In the refrigerator, you will find some cookies.**

- Perhaps, you are shopping for someone else and see the item **Eyes kreme** on the list. What do you buy? Ice cream? Or perhaps cream for eyes? By the way, your response to the above will reveal something about your own learning style. If you instantly chose "ice cream," you are probably an auditory learner; if you chose "cream for eyes," you probably learn best by using visual aids.

Remember that the purpose of ALL writing is communication, and if you are not able to write clear and effective sentences, then your reader may not understand what you are trying to say. Part III of this textbook will focus on building your sentence skills.

CHAPTER 9

The Basics: Parts of Speech

PARTS OF SPEECH

A surgeon may not necessarily know the names of all the tools he/she uses in the operating room. But as a patient, you probably want reassurance that she/he knows how to use them. The same can be said about parts of speech. You may never have to take a test to recognize and name the part of speech of EACH word in a sentence, but you need to know how to use the words correctly. The quality and effectiveness of your writing can depend on the words you choose to express your ideas. The following section is designed to help you review or become acquainted with the words that make up a sentence.

Nouns

Nouns are words that name people, places, things, and ideas. Nouns can be found anywhere in a sentence and often have articles (*a, an, the*) before them:

      noun   **noun**   **noun**   **noun**   **noun**
My *mother* works at *Food-4-Less* five *mornings* a *week* as a *cashier.*

      noun   **noun**   **noun**
Sacramento is the *capital* of *California.*

         noun   **noun**   **noun**
During the *Cold War,* the *United States* tried to stop the *spread* of

      noun
communism.

Adjectives

Adjectives are words that modify nouns and pronouns. Most adjectives answer the questions *What kind? Which one?* and *How Many?*

- Adjectives that answer the *What kind?* question describe the noun or pronoun. They tell the quality, condition, or kind of noun or pronoun.

black horse   *dirty* shoes
quiet children   *angry* teacher
The sky is *blue.*   The *red* and *black* ball is mine.

- Adjectives that answer the *Which one?* question restrict the meaning of a noun. Some of these adjectives are pronouns that function as adjectives.

my sister   *our* homework   *other* parents
this computer   *those* classrooms

- Adjectives that answer the *How many?* question are numbering words.

four chairs   *some* string beans   *each* student
few pennies   *fifty-five* dollars   *one* pallet

The three articles *a, an,* and *the* are adjectives that indicate nouns.

A student ate *an* apple for lunch in *the* cafeteria.

Pronouns

Pronouns are words that replace nouns.

- Some pronouns may represent specific persons or things:

I	she	they	you
me	her	them	yourself
myself	herself	themselves	yourselves
it	he	we	who
itself	him	us	whom
that	himself	ourselves	

- Some pronouns show possession:

my	our	your	his
her	their	its	

- Indefinite pronouns refer to nouns in a general way:

each	everyone	nobody	somebody

- Other pronouns cite particular things:

Singular	**Plural**
this, that	these, those
This is my house	*These* are my children.
That is Tom's car.	*Those* are my dogs.

- Some pronouns introduce questions:
  Which is the best car to buy?
  What shall I cook for dinner tonight?
  Who is going to the fair?

- Pronouns can be found anywhere within a sentence:

        pn   **pn**   **pn**
  Jose loaned *his* car to *his* sister so that *she* could go to work.

        pn
  The children played outside for an hour before *they* ate lunch.

  pn   **pn**   **pn**
  My daughter gave *herself* a pedicure after *she* came home from school.

Verbs

Verbs reflect action or state of being of subjects. Verbs also show tense or when something happened.

- Action verbs are pretty easy to find:
  The lioness *chased* and *caught* a wildebeest.
  The lioness *shared* her prey with the pride of lions.

- The being verbs include such verbs as *is, was, are, am,* and *were.*

       v
  That man *is* my English teacher.

          v
  The children *were* up very early this morning.

- The form of a verb expresses its tense or time of action. Two common tenses are present and past.

       v
  Xia *walks* most every morning between six and seven.

         v
  Yesterday, Xia *slept* until eight, however.

- Helping verbs used with the main verb form other tenses. The combination of verbs is called a verb phrase.

        v   **v**   **hv**
  Morgan *bought* a dress yesterday, but it *has* a defect, so she *will*

    v
  return it today.

        v   **hv** **hv** **v**
  Thomas *stayed* up last night to study so that he *would be ready* for his test.

Some helping verbs can be used as main verbs too: *has, have, had, is, am, are, was,* and *were.* Other helping verbs are only helpers: *could, would, will, shall,* and *should.*

- Verbs usually come after a sentence's subject except when a question is asked.

        hv   **v**
  Suzanne *will arrive* tomorrow.

    hv   **v**
  Will Suzanne *arrive* tomorrow?

- Words ending in -ing must have a helping verb in order to function as the verb of a sentence.

        hv   **v**
  The sleeping baby *is taking* a long nap.

                v
  After taking a long nap, the baby *was* in a good mood.

- Do not confuse infinitives with verbs. Infinitives are verbals that use the word "to" followed by the simple form of a verb.

       v
  Maria *wanted* to buy a new computer.

       v
  Tomas *needed* to go to the store to buy some milk.

Adverbs

Adverbs modify verbs, adjectives, and other adverbs. Adverbs answer the questions *How? Where? When* and *To what degree?*

- Modifying a verb:

     v   **adv**
  Harjit *mowed* the lawn <u>quickly</u>.

- Modifying an adjective:

      v **adv** **adj**
  The children *were* <u>very</u> happy.

- Adverbs that answer the How? question reflect how something is done.
  Bob <u>greedily</u> counted the money in his wallet.
  Noreen ate her food <u>noisily</u>.

- Adverbs that answer the Where? question show location.
  They lived <u>uptown</u>.
  The students climbed <u>upstairs</u>.

- Adverbs that answer the When? question express time.
  <u>Tomorrow</u>, I plan to do some housework.
  It is raining <u>today</u>.

- Adverbs that answer the To what degree? question reveal extent.
  Juan was <u>very</u> happy with his purchase.
  Connie was <u>somewhat</u> surprised with her test score.

- Most words ending in -ly are adverbs, but some are not.

  adv
  The student <u>tactfully</u> worded his question.

  adj
  He hid the <u>ugly</u> toys.

- One group of adverbs is called conjunctive adverbs. Some common conjunctive adverbs are the following:

also	however	indeed	moreover
nevertheless	therefore	consequently	otherwise
then	thus	instead	

  I like many vegetables. *However,* I hate carrots.
  Dhavel dislikes spinach and squash; *otherwise* he likes all vegetables.

Prepositions

Prepositions are words that connect. Prepositional phrases are made up from a preposition followed by its object (a noun) and its modifiers (usually adjectives or pronouns functioning as adjectives).

p adj noun
Joan bought some groceries <u>at</u> the store.

p   adj   noun p adj noun
Tommy took a picture <u>of</u> a beautiful tree for his class.

- Below are some of the most common prepositions:

about	before	by	into	past
above	behind	despite	like	to
across	below	down	near	toward
after	beneath	during	of	under
against	beside	for	off	until
among	between	from	on	upon
around	beyond	in	over	with

- Some prepositions consist of more than one word and contain other parts of speech:

according to	as far as	because of	in spite of
ahead of	as well as	in back of	instead of
along with	aside from	in front of	together with

In spite of a bull market, John lost money in his stock portfolio.

- Do not confuse prepositions with adverbs.
  Tina walked <u>across the room</u> slowly. (preposition with an object)
  Tina walked <u>across</u> slowly. (adverb without an object)

Conjunctions

Conjunctions connect and show relationships between words, phrases, and clauses. A phrase is a group of words—*to sink in the middle of the pool*, for example. A clause is a group of words that has a subject and a verb. There are two types of clauses: independent and dependent. An independent clause can stand alone as a sentence: Nora read her book. A dependent clause cannot stand alone as a sentence: When Nora read her book. There are two types of conjunctions: coordinating and subordinating conjunctions.

- **Coordinating conjunctions** include the following seven words: for, and, nor, but, or, yet, so.

  If you put the conjunctions' first letters together, they spell FANBOYS, an acronym many teachers use to help their students to remember the coordinating conjunctions. Coordinating conjunctions connect words, phrases, and clauses that are equal in importance:

  Tom bought a new car, *for* his old one quit running. (clauses)

  Margery *and* George dated for six months. (words)

  Hamilton does not eat breakfast, *nor* does he eat lunch. (clauses)

  Los Angeles is an interesting city, *but* its traffic is awful. (clauses)

  You can go to the dance *or* to the bowling ally. (phrases)

  Pam's dinner tasted good *yet* was not very filling. (phrases)

  Jasper studied for his midterm, *so* he passed it with a good grade. (clauses)

- **Subordinating conjunctions** connect dependent clauses to independent clauses. The following subordinating conjunctions are the most commonly used:

after	because	provided	whenever
although	before	since	where
as	but that	so that	whereas
as if	if	till	whenever
as long as	in order that	until	wherever
as soon as	notwithstanding		when

The following **relative pronouns** can also act as subordinating conjunctions.

| who | whose | whom |
| which | that | |

Use a comma at the end of a dependent clause if it comes before the independent clause. Do not use a comma if the dependent clause comes after the independent clause.

> Because Sarah was tired, she went to bed early. (comma needed)
>
> Sarah went to bed early because she was tired. (no comma)
>
> Sarah is one of those people who go to bed early every night. (no comma)

- Some words function as both conjunctions and prepositions: *after, for, since,* and *until.*

  > The man ate lunch *after he had worked four hours.* (conjunction)
  > The boy ran *after the ball.* (preposition)

EXERCISE 9A

DIRECTIONS: Identify the part of speech of the *italicized* words in the following.

1. On *her* way to the store, Carmen *stopped* by the post office to mail a *package.*
2. While at *the* post office, she saw her friend Mary, *and* the two of them decided to get a cup of *hot* coffee *at* the Coffee House.
3. *After* drinking her *coffee,* Carmen drove to Raley's *grocery* store.
4. She bought her week's *supply* of groceries and *then* drove *slowly* to her home.
5. *When she* arrived at her house, Carmen asked her *two* children to bring the groceries into her kitchen; they *grudgingly* did so.

DIRECTIONS: Identify the parts of speech in the following sentences: nouns (n), adjectives (adj), pronouns (pro), verbs (v), adverbs (adv), prepositions (p), coordinating conjunctions (cc), and subordinating conjunctions (sc).

1. The boy and girl shared their lunch every day.
2. Hannah bought some red and yellow apples at the store before she went to the post office.
3. The students tried to stay awake while they listened to their teacher's lecture, but some drifted off to sleep.
4. The grey border collie stared at the white sheep as it circled around the flock.
5. The woman furiously ironed her dress, so she could wear it for her interview.
6. However, she left the iron on one spot too long and burned the dress.
7. Juan was good in math, did all his homework, and passed the course with an *A*.
8. Harjit kicked the soccer ball and made a goal for his team.
9. The construction workers took a lunch break before they framed the house.
10. Nora, a very good friend of mine, moved to New York City last week.

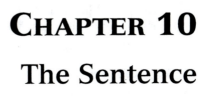

CHAPTER 10

The Sentence

Now that you know the names of some of the "tools" you use to create sentences, let us define exactly what a sentence is. A sentence should contain a subject and a verb. It should also express a complete thought. Why? Examine the following:

- I went to the party.
- After I went to the party.

Both of these word groups contain a subject (*I*) and a verb (**went**). However, if we read the second one, we are left with questions:

- What did I do after I went to the party?
- What happened after I went to the party?

The first word group is a sentence; the second one is a fragment because it is incomplete. See the end of this chapter for ways to recognize and fix fragments in your writing.

IDENTIFYING SUBJECTS AND VERBS

A simple explanation of what subjects and verbs do in a sentence is that the **subject** is what the sentence is about, and the verb shows what the subject is doing or being. This is a relatively easy task if the sentence is short and sweet:

- Frank cried.

Most of us would have no trouble looking at this sentence, asking the Who? or What? Questions, and coming up with the following:

- Who or what is the sentence about? **Frank.** Therefore **Frank** is the subject.
- What did Frank do? He **cried.** Therefore **cried** is the verb.

But of course, an essay filled with sentences of this length would be very boring. We usually add to the base sentence "Frank cried" lots of modifiers. We might actually write something like the following:

- In the afternoon, shortly after Mary walked out on him, Frank cried quietly in the corner of the garden.

With the addition of the extra words, the task of identifying subjects and verbs is not as clear cut. We need more tools to help.

Finding Subjects

- **Noun Subjects:** In many cases, the subject of a sentence is a noun.
  Frank cried.
  The **girl** ran to the park.
  Many **children** attend day care.

- **Pronoun Subjects:** The subject may also be a pronoun.
  He cried.
  She ran to the park.
  They attend day care.

- **Verbals as Subjects:**
  Swimming is my favorite summer pastime.
  To swim is Tom's greatest passion.

When a sentence is written in the pattern of subject/verb as all of the above examples are, the subject and verb are fairly easy to identify. But here are two special instances to consider.

- **Here is/There are constructions:**
  When a sentence begins with "here is/are" or "there is/are," the subject comes AFTER the verb.

      Verb   **Subject**
  Here is a good example.

      Verb   **Subject**
  There are three cute puppies in my backyard.

- **Commands:**
  When the sentence is a command, the subject is an implied you.
  [*You*] Find the good example.
  [*You*] Stop.

- **Other subjects to consider:**
  Sometimes, there may be two—or more—subjects to go with one verb.
  Mary, Fred, and Alice cried.
  Swimming, jogging, and hiking are my favorite activities in the summer.

  As *Mary, Fred,* and *Alice* are all performing the action, all three are the subject. Similarly, as I have THREE favorite activities, *swimming, jogging,* and *hiking* are all the subject of the second sentence.

- **Questions:**

    You may need to reword—answer—the question to find the subjects.

    Where are you going? BECOMES You are going where.
    You is the subject and ***are going*** is the verb.

EXERCISE 10A

DIRECTIONS: Find the subjects in the following sentences.

Sentence	Subject
1. What do you want for Christmas?	_____
2. He went home.	_____
3. Juan and Maria sat at the table.	_____
4. Sit.	_____
5. Arguing is futile.	_____
6. Sanjeet, Corinne, and Alex decided to transfer to UCLA.	_____
7. My mother bakes a wonderful apple pie.	_____
8. After the party, I stumbled home.	_____
9. Can you see Cinnamon, the apricot poodle?	_____
10. Is that Cinnamon standing beside Annabelle, the black cat?	_____

Finding Verbs

Most students, when asked to define verbs, reply "an action word." But examine how ***run*** is used in the following sentences:

- We ***run*** in the park every Saturday.
    (*run is a verb,* subject *We*)
- We wanted to ***run*** in the park.
    (part of infinitive *to run* acting as object of the verb *wanted*)
- Next week, we have entered the fun ***run.***
    (noun, object of verb *have entered*)
- The ***run*** length of the movie is 120 minutes.
    (adjective modifying the noun *length*)
- Don't go into the dog **run.**
    (noun, object of preposition *into*)

Each of these sentences contains the "action" word ***run,*** but only in the first one does the word function as the verb of the sentence. Remember from the previous chapter on Parts of Speech that a verb preceded by "to" never functions as the verb of a sentence.

Action Verbs

Even though every action word is not necessarily a verb, many action words do indeed function as verbs. In the following sentences, all of the words in bold type indicate an action and all of these words function as the verb of the sentence.

- I **wrote** my essay the night before it was due.
- I **received** a *D* for the essay.
- The instructor **pointed** to all of the sentence errors in my essay.
- She **explained** the corrections needed.

Linking Verbs

However, action words are not the only words that function as verbs. A verb can also express a state of being. Look at the bolded words in the following sentences.

- I **am** sick about my essay grade.
- Tom, however, **is** happy with his *A*.

Such verbs are called linking verbs. They "link" the subject with either an adjective that describes the subject OR a noun that provides further information about the subject.

Subject	Linking Verb	Adjective
The twins	are	identical.
My mom	was	tired.
My teenage years	were	horrible.
My English class	is	fun.

Subject	Linking Verb	Noun
Jody and Joy	are	twins.
Patricia	is	my mom.
My teenage years	were	the worst years of my life.
My English class	is	a fun class.

Helping Verbs

There are other types of verbs to consider also. The verbs in the following sentences are **bolded.**

- I **wrote** my essay the night before it **was** due.
- I **received** a D for the assignment.

- My teacher **is** unreasonable.
- I **have written** many other essays the night before they **were** due.
- I **have** never **received** a D before.
- My previous teachers **have** never **been** unreasonable.
- I hope my future teachers **will** not **be** unreasonable.

Notice how the verbs in the last two sentences consist of two words. In these sentences, "have" is functioning as a helping verb to indicate time— when the event occurred.

PHRASES AND CLAUSES

Now that you know how to identify subjects and verbs, it should be easy to understand the difference between phrases and clauses.

Phrases

A phrase is a group of words that DOES NOT contain a subject and a verb.

- Running in the park.
- To run in the park.
- In the park.
- At work.
- The boy with the blond hair.

Here are the most common types of phrases:

Prepositional phrase

This phrase begins with a preposition (see Parts of Speech section for a chart of these words) and ends with a noun or a pronoun.

- In the park
- At work
- With the blond hair.

Here is how these phrases might function in a sentence:

- He is running *in the park.*
- The boy *with the blond hair* is my brother.

Infinitive phrase

Infinitive phrases will contain a *to* followed by a verb and sometimes a verb and a noun. Remember that these phrases do not act as the verb of a sentence.

- I wanted *to go home.* (object of the verb *wanted*)

- I wanted *to leave.* (object of the verb *wanted*)
- *To go home* is my greatest dream. (subject of verb *is*)

Participial phrase

These phrases begin with the participial form of the verb (the -ing or -ed form)

- Running in the park, Tom fell down.
- Wanting some grapes, I went to the store.
- Tired of my classes, I left school for the day.
- Frustrated with my job, I quit.

Clauses

A clause consists of a group of words that DOES contain a subject and a verb.

- I went to the party.
- After I went to the party.

In both of the above examples, **I** is the subject and **went** is the verb. However, as previously discussed, the second clause is not a complete thought because it leads to the question "What happened?" Obviously, then, there are different types of clauses.

Independent Clauses (I.C.)

An independent clause can stand alone—it is therefore a sentence.

- I went to the party.
- Jose graduated from Sacramento High School.
- Maria and Joseph will receive scholarships to UCLA.

Dependent Clauses (D.C.)

A dependent clause can not stand alone. A dependent clause begins with a subordinating conjunction OR a relative pronoun. Refer to Chapter 9 for a list of these words.

- Since I went to the party.
- Because Jose graduated from Sacramento High School.
- Unless Maria and Joseph receive scholarships to UCLA.

EXERCISE 10B

DIRECTIONS: Identify the following groups of words as either an independent clause (I.C.), a dependent clause (D.C.), or a phrase (PH).

_____ 1. The best apple pie in the world.

_____ 2. My mom bakes the best apple pie in the world.

_____ 3. Unless my mom bakes an apple pie.

_____ 4. Wanting to go home.

_____ 5. Under the table.

_____ 6. Who is standing on the corner?

_____ 7. Sick and tired of school.

_____ 8. Trying hard to do my homework.

_____ 9. I tried hard to do my homework.

_____10. Please do your homework.

RECOGNIZING AND FIXING FRAGMENTS

Many students include fragments (non sentences) in their writing. Now that you can recognize the difference between a phrase and a clause, identifying fragments should be a lot easier. A fragment is a group of words that is punctuated as a sentence (capital letter at the beginning, period at the end) but which is not a sentence.

> Yesterday, ten students were absent from class. Because there was an assignment due.

> "Because there was an assignment due." is a fragment.

Fixing Fragments

Fragments are relatively easy to fix. You have three choices.

- Attach the fragment to the sentence before it.

Incorrect:	The woman furiously ironed her dress. So she could wear it for her interview.
Correct:	The woman furiously ironed her dress, so she could wear it for her interview.

- Attach the fragment to the sentence after it.

  | **Incorrect:** | Trying hard to stay awake during the lecture. Samantha finally fell asleep on her desk. |
  | **Correct:** | Trying hard to stay awake during the lecture, Samantha finally fell asleep on her desk. |

- Make the fragment into a complete sentence.

  | **Incorrect:** | Toddlers often need a nap in the afternoon. And sometimes in the morning as well. |
  | **Correct:** | Toddlers often need a nap in the afternoon. They sometimes need one in the morning as well. |

Identifying Fragments

Even though fragments are easy to fix, they still appear consistently in many students' essays. Why? Fragments are not easy to recognize in your own writing. Here are some warning signs to look for.

- **-*ing* and *to* fragments:**
  - ***Wanting to go to the party.*** I bought a new dress.
  - ***To play baseball.*** Is Frank's greatest wish.
  - ***Before eating dinner.*** Be sure to wash your hands.

- **Dependent word fragments:**
  - Because I wanted to go to the party.
  - Since Frank wanted to play baseball.
  - If you want to enjoy your dinner.

- **Added Detail fragments:**
  - Such as apples, oranges, pears, and bananas.
  - For example, running, jogging, and playing tennis.

- **Missing Subject fragments:**
  - The twins wanted to go to the baseball game. ***And then go out to dinner.***
  - My father promised us that we could all have a toy. ***But not play with it until after dinner.***

If you can identify the type(s) of fragments in your writing, it will be easy to fix them using one of the three methods mentioned above.

EXERCISE 10C

Identifying and Correcting Fragments

DIRECTIONS: Identify and fix any fragments in the following groups.

1. Three little girls were playing in the sandbox. One filling a pail and the other two digging a hole. They were trying to build a pretend town with the sand.

2. The man was shopping in the grocery store. He needed food for dinner, and he wanted to make a cake for dessert. Although, he had never baked before.
3. Connie was mad at herself because she had left some things at her friend's house. Her new book, some make-up, and her wallet. Now she had to go get them because she needed them tomorrow morning.
4. Plugging his role on *Third Watch*. Tom Berenger was on *The View* this week. NBC must be using him to boost *Third Watch's* ratings because he was on *The Tonight Show* too.
5. Jose was covered in grease. Because he had been working on his car all day. Luckily, he was wearing old clothes.

EXERCISE 10D

Identifying and Correcting Fragments

DIRECTIONS: Identify and fix any fragments in the following paragraphs.

Afraid of their teacher Mr. Kelley. The students nervously walked into the classroom and sat down. A few students talked quietly, but most were silent. Mr. Kelley quickly walked into the room. And set his notes on the lectern. At exactly nine, he called roll, sneering every time a student was absent. Then he began his lesson. "Any questions about the essay you read last night?" he asked. No one dared to ask a question, so all the students were silent. "Then let me ask a question," Mr. Kelly said. "What is the author's thesis?" Everyone looking at his or her book and no one saying anything. Finally, Calvin said the thesis was the first sentence. "The first sentence?" Mr. Kelly asked. "How can the thesis be the first sentence when it is a question?" Silence again. Then Dao said the thesis is the answer to the question. Mr. Kelly smiled and told his students to answer the question. Dao was the first to come up with an answer, and Mr. Kelly said she was right. Finally, Mr. Kelly told the students to list the support for the thesis and to turn in their work before the class was over. The students were relieved when the class was over. Because they did not have to deal with Mr. Kelly any more.

CHAPTER 11

Sentence Variety

Whenever we write, we need to think of sentence variety because our readers will be bored quickly if they read the same type—and length—of sentence over and over. Imagine, reading five pages of an essay that begins like this:

> Yesterday, I got out of bed. Then, I had breakfast. Then, I had a shower. Then I went to school. Then I went to work . . .

Your prose needs to "flow" smoothly, with peaks and valleys to help emphasize your ideas. There are various techniques you can use to retain your reader's attention and make your writing more effective.

TYPES OF SENTENCES

Perhaps the best way to write sentences with a variety of structures is first to become familiar with the four basic types of sentences: simple, compound, complex, and compound-complex.

Simple Sentence

- A simple sentence is made up with just one independent clause:

  s   v

  My brother watches too much television.

- Simple sentences may have compound subjects and compound verbs also.

  s   s v   v

  The boy and girl ate lunch and watched TV.

- Simple sentences can be short or long depending upon your need. To write longer simple sentences, we can add phrases:

  prep   infinitive   prep

  Noreen drove <u>to the store</u> <u>to buy</u> some bread <u>for her children's lunch</u>.

      adjective   **prep**

<u>Twirling her thumbs</u>, Connie did not pay attention <u>to her mother</u>.

    absolute   **infinitive**

<u>Arms waving</u> madly, Andy wanted <u>to get</u> his teacher's attention.

    infinitive   **prep**   **prep**

<u>To get up</u> <u>on time</u> <u>in the morning</u>, Andrew used three alarm clocks.

      appositive   **prep**

Maria, <u>my best friend</u>, drove me <u>to school</u> each day.

Compound Sentence

Compound sentences contain two or more independent clauses that are connected by coordinating conjunctions or semicolons.

  s   **v**   **cc** **s**   **v**

Bill stayed up late studying for his test, but he failed it anyway.

  s   **v**   **v**   **s**   **v**

Corey did not study for his test; however, he received a "B."

  s   **v**   **cc** **s**   **v**   **v**

Maria wanted to bake a cake, but she did not have any flour.

  s   **v**   **s**   **v**

Lucille wanted to be a doctor; therefore, she became a premed student.

Complex Sentence

Complex sentences have an independent and a dependent clause. Dependent clauses begin with a subordinating conjunction. If the dependent clause begins the sentence, set it off with a comma.

         s   **v**   **s**   **v**   **v**

Because Dan always hit the girls in his class, Shannon did not like him.

  s   **v**   **s**   **v**

Connie cried *after* she stubbed her toe.

    s   **v**   **s**   **v**

When Xia bought her new car, she paid a small price for it.

     s   **v**   **s**   **v**

Although Maria was a vegetarian, she sometimes ate poultry.

Compound-Complex Sentence

Compound-complex sentences have two independent clauses and one dependent clause. A coordinating conjunction or a semicolon connects the two independent clauses.

         s   v   s   v   v

Although Tom hated to get grease on his hands, he did not have enough

                          cc s   v

money to take his car to Jiffy Lube, so he changed the oil himself.

   s   v   cc s   v   s   v

Bill hated the color green, but he wore green today *because* it was St.
Patrick's Day.

     s   v   s   v   s

Annabelle bought herself a new dress; *when* she arrived home, she

   v   v

did not like it any more.

     s   v   s   v   v

When Nora married Helmut, she did not believe in divorce; after

               s   v

three years together, they divorced each other.

EXERCISE 11A

DIRECTIONS: Combine the following sentences in three different ways
as indicated. Make sure you retain all ESSENTIAL information.

> Koalas are cute.
> Koalas are cuddly.
> Koalas have sharp claws.

Simple: _____

_____

Compound: _____

_____

Complex: _____

_____

EXERCISE 11B

DIRECTIONS: Combine the following sets of sentences into one sentence—
either a simple, compound, complex, or compound-complex sentence.

1. Bob's tennis shoes had holes in them. He needed new tennis shoes.
   He bought a new pair of tennis shoes. The new pair was from Pay-
   less Shoes.
2. The students were not reading their assigned work. Their teacher
   was Mr. Smith. Mister Smith was mad. He wanted to give them a
   quiz. The quiz was a punishment.

3. The Dinner Party scam is a pyramid. Pyramids are illegal. This latest scam involves people giving $5,000 to a person at the top of a list of people. The list contains 56 names. People at the bottom of the list don't have a chance to win any money.

4. The baseball game was tied. The score was 6 to 6. It was the ninth inning. The home team was up to bat. The first hitter hit a home run. His score won the game for his team.

5. Cecilia wanted to throw a strike. She had thrown all strikes up to that point. A strike would give her a perfect game. She did not throw a strike.

OTHER CONSIDERATIONS

Just including some different types of sentences in your writing may not be enough to provide rhythm. Imagine, for instance if Brent Staples had opened his essay "Black Men and Public Space" with the following paragraph.

A. My first victim was a woman and she was white. She was also well dressed and she was probably in her late twenties. I came upon her late one evening. It was on a deserted street in Hyde Park. Hyde Park is a relatively affluent neighborhood. And it is in an otherwise mean, impoverished section of Chicago. As I swung onto the avenue behind her, there seemed to be a discreet uninflammatory distance between us. I soon found out that there was not a distance between us. This woman looked at me and saw a youngish black man. She saw a man who is six feet two inches and broad of build, and he has a beard. He also has billowing hair, and both of his hands were shoved into the pockets of a bulky military jacket. I could tell that I seemed menacingly close to her. After she looked at me a few more times, she picked up her pace. She was soon running in earnest, and she soon disappeared into a cross street.

Staples' language is effective; he uses words like ***impoverished, uninflammatory,*** and ***billowing,*** and these may well have been the sentences he used in the first draft of his essay. But now read the introduction that actually appears in the finished product:

B. My first victim was a woman—white, well dressed, probably in her late twenties. I came upon her late one evening on a deserted street in Hyde Park, a relatively affluent neighborhood in an otherwise mean, impoverished section of Chicago. As I swung onto the avenue behind her, there seemed to be a discreet, uninflammatory distance between us. Not so. She cast back a worried glance. To her, the youngish black man—a broad six feet two inches with a beard and billowing hair, both hands shoved into the pockets of a bulky military jacket—seemed menacingly close. After a few more quick glimpses, she picked up her pace and was soon running in earnest. Within seconds she disappeared into a cross street.

Few people would argue that this second paragraph is much more rhythmic, much more sophisticated. Let us examine the second paragraph more closely.

Sentence Length

If all of your sentences are a similar length, your ideas may seem like a list. Note in paragraph **B** how Staples' sentences vary in length as follows

1. 14 words	5. 6 words
2. 26 words	6. 32 words
3. 18 words	7. 17 words
4. 2 words	8. 9 words

We can almost visualize the "hills and valleys" that keep the reader moving through the paragraph. Following a long sentence with a short one can be particularly useful when emphasizing a point.

Adding Questions and Intentional Fragments

Note also how Staples uses the short fragment "not so" to emphasize the idea that, even though he assumed there was enough distance between him and the woman so that she wouldn't be afraid, the opposite was true.

**Note: Check with your instructor before you use intentional fragments in your essays.

Writers also include questions to add rhythm. Note how Barbara Ascher includes questions—and intentional fragments—in the following paragraph from "On Compassion."

> Twice I have witnessed this, and twice I have wondered, what compels this woman to feed this man? Pity? Care? Compassion? Or does she simply want to rid her shop of his troublesome presence? If expulsion were her motivation she would not reward his arrival with gifts of food. Most proprietors do not. They chase the homeless from their midst with expletives and threats.

Sentence Openings

Another way to avoid "listing" your ideas is to vary the beginnings of your sentences. Don't for instance, begin every sentence with subject followed by verb:

I went . . .
My mother thought . . .
Several people agreed . . .

Instead, try beginning some sentences with prepositional phrases (Chapter 9), some with dependent clauses (Chapter 11), some with transitional words/phrases (Chapter 2).

Don't Underestimate the Use of the "Simple" Sentence

Remember that a "simple" sentence is not necessarily one that is short; simple only means that there is one independent clause. Of the eight sentences in paragraph B above, six of them are simple sentences. Note how Staples imbeds different *types of phrases* into his work.

- My first victim was a woman—*white, well dressed, probably in her late twenties.*
- To her, the youngish black man—*a broad six feet two inches with a beard and billowing hair, both hands shoved into the pockets of a bulky military jacket*—seemed menacingly close.

EXERCISE 11C

Revising for Sentence Variety and Style

DIRECTIONS: Using the techniques discussed above, revise the following paragraph.

The world is a vastly different place than it was when I was a kid. Times have to change. Things seem to have changed drastically in the last fifteen years or so. These changes have been much like earthquakes. They have been entirely unexpected and have done some serious damage. One of these changes is the boom in technology of the latter half of the twentieth century. It's amazing what has been done with computers in the last several decades. They have gone from being huge, cumbersome, machines to portable, efficient, devices. These devices can be used at home, at work, at school, and even at the local coffee shop. The astronomical increase in the use of computers has its positive effects. There are also many negatives as well. One of these negatives is the drastic increase in the occurrence of identity theft. People's identities are being stolen far more frequently than ever before. It's largely due to the easy access to others personal information, including names, addresses, social security numbers and credit card numbers. Internet-related identity theft has caused much damage to many peoples credit ratings and lives.

CHAPTER 12

Writing Correct Sentences

RUN-ONS AND COMMA SPLICES

As previously mentioned, a **sentence** contains at least one subject and at least one verb, and it must be a complete thought (independent clause). You have also seen how two independent clauses can be combined to make longer, more "flowing" sentences. Many writers, wanting to make their sentences longer and more varied, may join independent clauses incorrectly, either by using commas incorrectly (a comma splice) or not using any punctuation at all (a run-on).

Read the following sentences aloud to yourself:

> Students are usually stressed at the end of the semester they are worried about their final exams.

> I hate driving on the freeway the traffic is always very heavy.

> Cats are easy pets to have they are very self-sufficient.

> Jeff can't afford his rent he has to get a second job.

As you read, you probably noticed that each of these sentences is comprised of two complete thoughts, and/or that there is no "pause" between the two thoughts, thus causing them to "run together." The above sentences are examples of **run-ons.** The lack of punctuation in them makes it difficult for the reader to distinguish between the two separate thoughts in the sentence.

Now look at the same sentences again:

> Students are usually stressed at the end of the semester, they are worried about their final exams.

> I hate driving on the freeway, the traffic is always very heavy.

> Cats are easy pets to have, they are very self-sufficient.

> Jeff can't afford his rent, he has to get a second job.

You probably noticed that in each of the above sentences, commas have been inserted between the two independent clauses. Although this may *seem* more correct because there is now a pause between the two independent clauses, the addition of the commas has simply created a slightly different type of error, a **comma splice.**

Remember: Two independent clauses cannot be joined without any punctuation whatsoever, but they cannot be joined with just a comma either.

Fixing Run-Ons and Comma Splices

So how can you fix run-ons and comma splices in your writing? The following are a few ways in which two independent clauses can be joined effectively to create a sentence: .

- **Using a comma and a coordinating conjunction (for, and, nor, but, or, yet, so):**
  Choose the coordinating conjunction that best emphasizes the relationship between the two independent clauses. Remember that the comma goes **before** the coordinating conjunction. Here are the sentences above joined with a comma and a coordinating conjunction:

  Students are usually stressed at the end of the semester, for they are worried about their final exams.

  I hate driving on the freeway, for the traffic is always very heavy. (OR: The traffic is always very heavy, so I hate driving on the freeway.)

  Cats are very self-sufficient, so they are easy pets to have.

  Jeff can't afford his rent, so he has to get a second job. (OR: Jeff has to get a second job, for he can't afford his rent.)

- **Using a semicolon between the two independent clauses:**
  The semicolon is a very versatile punctuation mark; it is a sort of "half-comma, half-period" that can be used to create a "pause" between two independent clauses without actually beginning a new sentence. The semicolon can be used alone, but in some cases the use of a **conjunctive adverb** (*thus, therefore, however, nevertheless, consequently,* etc.) is even more effective in emphasizing the relationship between the ideas expressed in the two independent clauses. Here again are the original sentences joined with semicolons:

  Students are usually stressed at the end of the semester; they are worried about their final exams.

  The traffic is always very heavy; consequently, I hate driving on the freeway.

  Cats are very easy pets to have; they are very self-sufficient.

  Jeff can't afford his rent; therefore, he has to get a second job.

These are the two main ways to avoid run-ons and comma splices when joining independent clauses. You may also simply put a period after the first independent clause and make two sentences, but whenever possible, you should try to combine sentences to avoid an abundance of short, choppy sentences in your writing.

- **Using a subordinating conjunction to make one of the two statements into a dependent clause:**
  A subordinating conjunction (such as *although, because, unless, if, even though, since, while, etc.*) can be used to subordinate (deemphasize) one of the two ideas and place emphasis on the other. Be sure to use the subordinating conjunction that best shows the relationship between the two ideas. Again, here are the original sentences joined using subordination:

  > Students are usually stressed at the end of the semester because they are worried about their final exams.

  > I hate driving on the freeway because the traffic is always very heavy.

  > Because cats are very self-sufficient, they are very easy pets to have.

  > Since Jeff can't afford his rent, he has to get a second job.

Identifying Run-Ons and Comma Splices

Using any of the techniques described above, you should easily be able to fix any run-ons and/or comma splices in your writing. However, identifying them may not be so simple. Here are some tools to help.

Pronouns

Pronouns account for almost 85% of run-ons and comma splices in student writing. Why? Look at the following sentences

> My dog is an apricot poodle. He is called Cinnamon.

When we read these two sentences, we look at the concrete noun subject of the first sentence, **dog,** and we know that the pronoun subject **he** refers to **dog.** Often, then, when we write ideas like these, our minds recognize the connection between pronoun and noun and we group the two sentences together.

> My dog is an apricot poodle he is called Cinnamon.

However, the above is a run-on. Adding a comma doesn't help because a comma is not strong enough to join two sentences.

> My dog is an apricot poodle, he is called Cinnamon.

But now you know that this error can be fixed in the following ways:

My dog is an apricot poodle; he is called Cinnamon.
Because my dog is an apricot poodle, he is called Cinnamon.
My dog, an apricot poodle, is called Cinnamon.

Conjunctive adverbs

The second most common type of run-on or comma splice, occurs when the writer uses a conjunctive adverb to join two independent clauses.

My dog is an apricot poodle, also he is called Cinnamon.
My dog is an apricot poodle, therefore, he is called Cinnamon.

See the list of conjunctive adverbs in Chapter 9.

Added details

Even though run-ons and comma splices occur most often when the second sentence begins with a pronoun or a conjunctive adverb, there are other common causes. Often when we add details, we create an error.

Allen brought some of his favorite books on vacation with him, for example he brought *Harry Potter, The Green Mile, Lord of the Rings,* and *The Adventures of Huckleberry Finn.*

Contradictions

Often, when the sentence provides a contradiction, we fuse the two sentences together.

Allen brought some of his favorite books on vacation with him, he didn't bring any school books.

I always thought I would buy a two-storey house in the suburbs, I was wrong.

Both of the following comma splices could easily be fixed by adding a *but* after the comma.

Correcting Run-ons and Comma Splices

DIRECTIONS: Each of the following sentences is either a run-on or a comma splice. In the blank next to the sentence, indicate "RO" if the sentence is a run-on and CS if it is a comma splice. Then, correct the run-ons and comma splices using one of the methods explained in this section.

_____ 1. Gail drives an SUV, she considers herself to be an environmentalist.

_____ 2. My parents asked me what I wanted for my birthday, they didn't listen to my answer.

_____ 3. Kauai is my favorite of the Hawaiian islands it's less crowded than the others.

_____ 4. Josh is a big baseball fan, he never misses a Major League game.

_____ 5. I didn't bring my umbrella the weather forecast called for sunshine today.

_____ 6. Sacramento is the American city with the most trees per person, it has a lot of shade.

_____ 7. The best place to look for furniture is at garage sales, people get rid of a lot of really nice things.

_____ 8. Fighting the rush-hour traffic is not my idea of a productive morning, I walk to work instead.

_____ 9. Melissa bought a new stereo system for her car she has not yet figured out how it works.

_____ 10. Next year I will travel to Europe, I need to see the United States first.

More Correcting Run-ons and Comma Splices

DIRECTIONS: The paragraph below contains ten (10) run-ons and comma splices. Re-write the paragraph, correcting the run-ons and comma splices in one of the ways discussed in this section.

If you want a pet that is a good friend and easy to care for, consider getting a cat. First of all, cats are quiet, they don't bark and whine like dogs do. Your neighbors will never know you even have a pet, they will not have any reason to complain. Also, cats are very clean animals, they can be trained to use a litter box. They do not need to be taken outside to go to the bathroom you will not be awakened at 3:00 A.M. to let them out. And, cats generally don't require baths they bathe themselves and groom their own fur. They do not need a lot of exercise either, this makes less work for their owners. They do not need to be walked, just a few toys will keep them entertained and happy for hours. Cats are self-sufficient as well, they can survive being left alone for up to several days as long as they are given an adequate supply of food and water. Perhaps most importantly, in spite of their reputation for being aloof, cats can be very lovable pets, they are often cuddly and affectionate. Their reputation for aloofness probably stems from the fact that they are very independent creatures, it often seems like they don't really need people. Overall, cats make very good companions and virtually worry-free pets.

CORRECTING PRONOUN ERRORS

Chapter 9 of this Handbook describes a pronoun as a word that takes the place of a noun, but it will be easier to identify and fix pronoun errors in your writing if you are more aware of the particular functions that pronouns play in a sentence.

Pronoun Case

Look at the following sentences and note the pronouns used to replace the nouns.

    He   **her**
1. *Tom* went to the party with *Mary*.

    She   **him**
2. *Mary* went to the party with *Tom*.

      They
3. *Tom and Mary* went to the party.

      his
4. Mary went to *Tom's* party.

      her
5. Tom went to *Alice's* party

       their
6. Alice went to *Tom and Mary's* party.

      them
7. Alice went with *Tom and Mary* to the party.

The noun Tom is replaced by *he* in the first sentence, but *him* in the second sentence and *his* in the fourth. Moreover, when *Tom* is combined with *Mary* in the sixth sentence, we choose the pronoun *their.* Why? Because the choice of pronoun depends on the CASE of the noun. For instance, in sentence 1, we replace *Tom* with *he* because *Tom is the* **subject** of the sentence. In sentence 2, however, *Tom* is the object of the preposition *with,* so we choose the **objective** case. And in the fourth sentence, the noun *Tom* is followed by *'s,* indicating that Tom is **possessive.**

Subject Pronouns

I   she   he   it   they   you   who

Object Pronouns

me   her   him   it   them   you   whom

Possessive Pronouns

my   her   his   its   their   your   our   whose

When replacing a noun with a pronoun, always use the correct **case.**

Pronoun Reference

If a pronoun replaces a noun, there must be a noun to which your pronoun CLEARLY refers. This noun is usually called the antecedent. If there is not a clear antecedent, your sentence may be confusing. Examine the following sentences:

- Alison stopped buying her vegetables at the corner market because they charged too much.
  (Who charges too much?)

- My brother wants to become a physician, but I'm not interested in it.
  (I'm not interested in what?)

- Gina told Jessica that she had gained weight.
  (Who had gained weight?)

All of these sentences are unclear because of pronoun reference problems. The sentences would be clearer if written the following way:

- Alison stopped buying her vegetables at the corner market because the owners charged too much.

- My brother wants to become a physician, but I'm not interested in becoming one.

- Gina told Jessica, "You've gained weight."
                    OR
  Gina told Jessica, "I've gained weight."

Pronoun Agreement

A pronoun must also agree in number with its antecedent. That is why we replaced ***Tom and Mary*** in sentence 7 with ***them.*** Note the following:

- The ***boys*** wanted to repair ***their*** bicycles during the break.
- Several ***students*** lost ***their*** books last semester.
- ***Alicia*** gave up ***her*** seat on the bus yesterday because ***she*** saw an elderly woman struggling with her packages.

A SINGULAR noun, such as Alicia, is replaced by a SINGULAR pronoun, ***she*** or ***her.***
PLURAL nouns, such as ***boys*** and ***students*** are replaced by PLURAL pronouns ***their, them.***

Now look at the following:

- A ***parent*** should not spank ***their*** child.
- A ***student*** should turn in ***their*** essay on time.

Chances are you will hear these types of pronoun errors in everyday speech. But you can see that the SINGULAR noun ***parent*** should not be replaced by a PLURAL pronoun ***their.***

Why is this type of error becoming more prevalent? Not too long ago (as recently as the 1950's), we had a "generic" pronoun ***he.*** And ***he*** was used to refer to all of us, whether we were ***he's*** or ***she's.*** Soon, we realized that not all of us are ***he's,*** so we began to be "politically correct" and write ***he or she*** instead of ***he.***

A parent should not spank his or her child.
A student should turn in her or his essay on time.

The use of the dual pronouns is fine if used in moderation, but a whole paragraph containing he/she or him/her can be VERY confusing, and in speech the use of both pronouns becomes particularly tiresome. So we started throwing in the plural pronoun to make life easier.

A parent should not spank their child.

However, the use of *their* is incorrect. So what are writers to do if they want to write grammatically correct sentences but don't want to get bogged down with too many dual pronouns? Simple. Change the antecedent.

- *Parents* should not spank *their* child.
- *Students* should turn in *their* essays on time.

Indefinite Pronouns

Many errors in agreement occur when we have pronouns that refer to indefinite pronouns. Read the following sentences.

The boy needs *to bring **his*** book to class.
The boys need to bring ***their*** books to class.
Everyone needs to bring ***their*** book to class.

The last sentence may sound fine to you because ***everyone*** feels like it should be plural. But note that the verb ***needs*** is used—correctly—the same verb form that we use when the subject is SINGULAR (***boy***).

Contrary to what we may think, most indefinite pronouns are considered SINGULAR.

Singular Indefinite Pronouns

each	everyone	nobody	somebody
either	neither	anyone	someone
no one	another	anybody	everybody
everyone	everything	little	much
something			

Plural Indefinite Pronouns

both	few	many	others
several			

Some indefinite pronouns may be either singular or plural, depending on the context.

Singular or Plural

all	any	more	none
some			

All of the cake was left. (singular)
All of the students were standing next to the bus. (plural)

Pronoun Point of View

Pronouns come in three different points of view as follows:

FIRST	I	we
SECOND	you	
THIRD	he, she, it, they	

Changing the point of view in your writing can be very confusing—and annoying—to your reader. Moreover, switching points of view can result in illogical statements. For instance, read the following sentence, imagining that Alice is speaking to Tom, as she says,

> "One reason *I* like visiting San Francisco is because *you* have so much to do there."

Why would *Alice* like San Francisco because *Tom* has a lot to do there? Similarly, look at the following sentence:

> *I* recently purchased an SUV. *You* never know when someone's going to drive recklessly, and *one* has a better view of the road from an SUV.

This sentence would make much more sense if the writer had said

> I recently purchased an SUV. I never know when someone's going to drive recklessly, and I have a better view of the road from an SUV.

You should usually not be used in academic writing because the reader becomes the person being addressed, and sometimes the result can be offensive. Imagine, an overweight English teacher, a single mom, reading the following:

> *You* should lose weight.
> *You* should not abuse your child.

And **one** is so stuffy that this word is also probably best avoided.

> *One* needs to take care of *one's* books if *one* wants to sell them back at the end of the semester.

EXERCISE 12C

Choosing correct pronouns

DIRECTIONS: Choose the correct pronoun for each of the following.

1. Yesterday, several students went to _____ school's annual carnival where _____ saw some clowns performing a juggling act.
2. Particularly when a clown is juggling knives, _____ needs to be very careful.

3. For instance, if the knife falls, _____ could really hurt someone who is not aware of the danger _____ is in.
4. And a parent _____ is attending the carnival with _____ children, needs to be particularly careful.
5. Young children often run away from _____ parents and could come too close to the clown.

EXERCISE 12D

Correcting pronoun errors

DIRECTIONS: Rewrite the following paragraph, correcting any pronoun errors. Remember to look for errors in case, reference, agreement, and point of view.

Maria and Linda went to the mall Wednesday morning because she needed a dress before her weekend date with Bill. They had been going steady for three months and planned to go to a dance Saturday night. You usually want to impress someone when one is going on a special date and this was no exception. She was hoping to find a sexy red dress but would settle for purple or black too. She didn't want to go shopping alone because a friend will usually say what's on their mind. She was one friend whom would also tell the truth. They checked out four stores before they got hungry and decided to eat lunch. Since they did not have a lot of money, they split a small pizza at Round Table—you can usually get a cheap meal at Round Table—and each had their own drink. They saw two friends, Jose and Jimmy, but they could not stay to chat. Afterwards, they went to Macy's. While her friend tried on some jeans and blouses, she searched through the dresses. She did not find a red dress that she liked, but she did find a beautiful black one that was not too expensive. She found her friend, and they decided to celebrate their purchases by sharing an ice cream sundae. She had just enough money for a small one. After eating their sundae, they drove to her house for a relaxing swim in their pool. It was a perfect ending to a good day.

CORRECTING SUBJECT—VERB AGREEMENT ERRORS

As you have learned from earlier sections of this Handbook, every sentence must have a **subject** and a **verb.** The subject and verb in every sentence must **agree** in number; that is, if a subject is **singular,** the verb must be singular as well. Likewise, if the subject is **plural,** the verb must also be plural.

My **homework** *keeps* me really busy after school and on weekends.

Children often *have* very vivid imaginations.

Note that singular verbs most often end in "s," while plural verbs do not.

Although it is usually clear whether a subject is singular or plural, there are some subjects that appear to be plural when in fact they are not. These subjects can be one of several types:

- **Collective nouns**
  These are nouns that, while they refer to a group of people or things, are considered to be one unit; therefore, they are singular. Some examples of collective nouns are *committee, jury, faculty, audience, class, team, army,* and *government.*

  The **committee** *meets* every Wednesday at 3:00 P.M.

  The **audience** *applauds* at the end of each song.

- **Indefinite pronouns**
  These are pronouns that are always considered singular even though they generally refer to unspecified people or things. Some examples of indefinite pronouns are *everyone, everything, someone, something, anyone, anything, each, nothing, no one* and *every.*

  Everyone *is* responsible for preserving the environment.

  Someone *has* found my missing backpack.

  Everything he says *is* a lie.

  Each of us *is* expected to abide by the law.

**Remember that some indefinite pronouns, such as *all, none, some,* and *any,* can be either singular OR plural, depending on the noun or pronoun referred to.

  All of my homework *is* finished. (In this sentence, "all" refers to "homework," which is singular, so the verb is singular.)

  All of my friends *are* college students. (In this sentence, "all" refers to "friends," which is plural, so the verb is plural.)

- **Nouns may appear to be plural because they end in "s," but they are singular in meaning.** Many plural nouns end in "s." Some nouns ending in "s" may appear to be plural but are actually considered singular because they count as one unit or subject. Some of these nouns are *news, mathematics, statistics, economics, physics, athletics, measles, and politics.*

  Mathematics *is* not my best subject.

  The **news** about the economy *is* not good.

- **If two subjects are joined by "and," the verb must be plural.**

  Jeff and Jerry *live* next door to me.

  Cats and dogs usually *don't* get along.

- **If two subjects are joined by "or" or "nor," the subject closest to the verb determines whether the verb is singular or plural.**

  Neither **Rick nor his friends** *attend* class regularly. (In this sentence, "friends" is closest to the verb, and since it is plural, the verb must be plural as well.)

  Either **my math teacher or my history teacher** *gives* a test every day. (In this sentence, "history teacher" is closest to the verb, so the verb must be singular.)

- **The verb must agree with the subject even if the subject comes AFTER the verb or if the sentence begins with "there" or "here."**

  Where *are* my new **shoes?**

  There *is* a strange **odor** coming from the refrigerator.

EXERCISE 12C

Subject Verb Agreement

DIRECTIONS: Circle the correct form of the verb, either singular or plural, depending on the subject of the sentence.

1. People often (don't/doesn't) realize the significant consequences of their words and actions.
2. Neither stress nor strange noises (keeps/keep) me awake at night.
3. Everything in the house (were/was) burned in the fire.
4. The jury (consist/consists) of seven men and five women.
5. Either my mom or my dad (picks/pick) me up after school each day.
6. All of my family members (live/lives) in Vermont.
7. There (is/are) too many people in this room.
8. Neither your words nor your actions (means/mean) anything to me.
9. Anyone who (want/wants) to go on the trip must pay a deposit by next Friday.
10. Politics (is/are) a subject I don't discuss with friends.

EXERCISE 12D

More Practice With Subject-Verb Agreement

DIRECTIONS: In the following paragraph, circle and correct the subject-verb agreement errors you find (Hint: there are 10).

People are always amazed at what an upbeat, cheerful person I am. Neither the rush-hour freeway traffic nor the long lines in the grocery store ruins my positive outlook. If the news on TV are bad, I don't let it get to

me; I simply remind myself that tomorrow is another day and that everything are going to be all right. Even my noisy neighbors doesn't bother me;
I just ignore them and turn my stereo up louder. Neither my friends nor
my family members understands how I can be so cheerful even when
everything seem to be going bad around me. One time, I was very sick with
the measles, and when my mom called to see if I was all right, I told her in
my most cheerful voice that I was fine. My mother was stunned; she commented, "Even the measles don't bother you. I can't believe it." There are
very few things which truly bothers me. One of these things are the rude-
ness I often see people displaying in public. If anything get me down, it is
seeing someone say or do something mean to another person. Otherwise,
I take life as it comes and try to keep a positive outlook.

CHAPTER 13

Writing with Clarity and Style

You may have read the quotation "the pen is mightier than the sword." This is no idle statement, for writers have considerable power in the words they choose to express ideas. It is worthwhile, then, for you think about this aspect of writing.

COMMONLY CONFUSED WORDS

In the English language, there are many words that sound alike but are spelled differently and have different meanings (i.e. *their* and *there*). These sound-alike words are called **homonyms,** and because they sound nearly identical when spoken, they are frequently confused in writing. Although unintentional substitution of "here" for "hear" will probably not prevent your reader from understanding what you are trying to say, these words are not interchangeable, and it is important to know the difference between them and when to use each of them. This section of the handbook will provide you with a list of commonly confused words and how to distinguish between them. The following is a list of the most commonly confused words:

allowed	Permitted; deemed acceptable	Dogs are not *allowed* in the park.
aloud	Using the voice; orally	Poetry should be read *aloud*.
are	Form of verb *to be*	You *are* my best friend.
our	Belonging to us (possessive pronoun)	A fire destroyed *our* house.
bare	Unclothed; uncovered	Don't go outside with *bare* feet.
bear	An omnivorous mammal (noun); to carry or abide (verb)	At the zoo, we saw a brown *bear*. I can't *bear* to spend another summer in the desert.

break	To separate by force (verb); an interruption or intermission (noun)	I *break* every pair of sunglasses I buy.
brake	A device for slowing or stopping a vehicle (noun); to use such a device to slow or stop a vehicle (verb)	The car isn't stopping properly because of problems with the *brakes*.
do	To perform or execute; to fulfill or complete	I *do* my grocery shopping late at night.
due	Owed; payable immediately or on demand	My rent is *due* on the first of each month.
here	Refers to physical location	*Here* is my homework.
hear	To perceive with the ear	I can't *hear* you.
it's	It is (contraction)	*It's* a beautiful day.
its	Belonging to it (possessive pronoun)	The cat chased *its* tail.
knew	Past tense of verb *to know*	I *knew* the answers, but I forgot them as soon as the test began.
new	Not old; recent	My *new* computer is much faster than my old one.
know	To perceive with the mind or senses	Do you *know* how to make sushi?
no	The opposite of the affirmative	*No,* you can't go to the party tonight.
there	Refers to physical location	My car is over *there*.
their	Belonging to them (possessive pronoun)	The boys forgot *their* bikes.
they're	They are (contraction)	*They're* not home right now.
threw	Past tense of *to throw*	The fire started when someone *threw* a lit cigarette out a car window.
through	In one side and out the other side; by means of	I have a fear of driving *through* tunnels.

past	Refers to time (noun)	My grandfather often reminisces about the *past*.
passed	Past tense of the verb *to pass*	I *passed* by your house on the way to school this morning.
to	In a direction toward (preposition)	We drove *to* San Diego for spring break.
too	In addition; also	Cats are my favorite pets, but I like dogs *too*.
two	The number after one	I have *two* favorite colors: blue and green.
where	Refers to physical location	*Where* are my shoes?
wear	To carry or have on one's person	Joe has to *wear* a uniform to work.
whether	Alternative possibilities; either	I will go to the party *whether* or not you go with me.
weather	The state of the atmosphere at a given time	The *weather* is supposed to be sunny for the next several days.
which	What particular one or ones	*Which* house is yours?
witch	A woman believed to practice sorcery, usually in folklore	The *witch* is a popular costume at Halloween.
who's	Who is (contraction)	*Who's* there?
whose	Belonging to who (possessive pronoun)	*Whose* keys are these?
write	To form letters and words by hand with an instrument such as a pen or pencil	Now that e-mail has become so popular, people rarely *write* letters anymore.
right	Conforming with justice or morality; true or correct	I was raised to believe that it isn't *right* to lie.

you're	You are (contraction)	*You're* not very talkative today.
your	Belonging to you (possessive pronoun)	Where is *your* backpack?

The following are words that do not sound exactly alike but are also frequently confused:

accept	To receive willingly	Will you *accept* my apology?
except	Other than	I like all vegetables *except* peas.
affect	To influence or change	Smoking can negatively *affect* one's health.
effect	Something brought about by a cause; a result	Lung cancer is just one potential *effect* of a longterm smoking habit.
choose	To select (present tense of verb to *choose*)	Before registering, students should *choose* the classes they want to take.
chose	Past tense of the verb *to choose*	Gary *chose* to go to the baseball game instead of going to dinner with his family.
lose	To be unable to find; to not be the winner in a contest or game	I always *lose* my car keys.
loose	Not tightly fastened or secured	Two of the lug nuts on the wheel were *loose*.
than	Used to introduce the second element in a comparison	I would rather go on a cruise *than* to Las Vegas.
then	At that time; next in time, space, or order	*Then*, something very strange happened.

we're	We are (contraction)	*We're* leaving promptly at 7:00.
were	Past tense of the verb *to be*	Thousands of people *were* lined up to buy tickets to the Sacramento Kings' season opener.

EXERCISE 13A

Finding Commonly Confused Words

DIRECTIONS: Using the charts on the preceding pages, circle the correct word(s) in the following sentences.

1. (There/Their) are many people who do not know how to manage (there/their) time effectively.
2. (Who's/Whose) car is blocking my driveway?
3. (It's/Its) no surprise that many states have (past/passed) laws restricting the use of cell phones in public places.
4. Many English teachers will not (except/accept) assignments from students who arrive late (to/too) class on the date the assignment is (do/due).
5. (Where/wear) is the remote control? (Its/It's) right (hear/here).
6. Unleashed dogs are not (allowed/aloud) in most parks in Sacramento; however, on any given day (they're/there) are dogs running (loose/lose) in many city parks.
7. I would much rather do my homework (then/than) clean my room.
8. My neighbors' lack of consideration has had a negative (affect/effect) on me; I never realized how much others' behavior can (affect/effect) us.
9. I don't (no/know) (weather/whether) or not I (passed/past) my math test; I'll find out tomorrow.
10. (Our/Are) family takes a vacation every year; this year, (were/we're) going to Florida.

CHOOSING APPROPRIATE LANGUAGE

When writing a rough draft, writers do not think about language because they are mainly concerned with getting their thoughts organized and expressed. When revising and editing their essays, writers need to look closely at their writing to make it concise and vigorous. To do so, they need to look out for some problems.

Redundancies

Redundancies are words, phrases, and clauses that repeat what has already been said. Thinking they are emphasizing their points, writers often repeat themselves and add unnecessary words. For example, a fact is true, so combining the two—a true fact—is redundant. The word *fact* by itself is just fine. Rather than writing *the purple car,* a writer may write *the car was purple in color.* Since *purple* is a color, it is not necessary to state *purple in color.*

Below are some other examples of redundancies. The redundant words are crossed out:

- Frequently, ~~many times~~ during the afternoon, toddlers become tired and need a nap.
- The students walk into the classroom, ~~where learning takes place~~.
- The lion ~~ran after or~~ chased the wildebeest.
- The ~~end~~ result of the meeting was that we re-evaluated the basic fundamentals of our policies.
- The ~~free~~ gift was an ~~unexpected~~ surprise.

In the first example, *frequently* means *many times,* so the writer needs to delete either the word or the phrase. The word *classroom* is a place *where learning takes place,* so the tagged on phrase is not needed. In the third example, the phrase *ran after* repeats the meaning of *chased,* and since *chased* is more vigorous than *ran after, chased* is kept. You should be able to recognize why the words have been crossed out in the last two sentences.

Empty and Inflated Phrases

Examine the following three-word sentence:
    Smoking is dangerous.

Now look at a "padded" version of the same sentence:
    It is commonly assumed that those people who partake of nicotine in the form of tobacco rolled in thin paper, lit at one end, inhaled through the lungs, and then out again via the mouth or nose, are doing something that could be damaging to themselves and those around them.

Note that the second sentence is now 39 words long and not an ounce of additional information has been added.

Students are often tempted when faced with a page requirement for an assignment to pad their ideas with empty and meaningless phrases in order to fulfill the assignment directions. Such essays are usually confusing and boring to both writer and reader. If you want to make your essays long, add more specific, concrete details. Avoid using the following "empty" phrases and words.

kind of	sort of	type of
basically	definitely	actually
type of	generally	individual
specific	really	particular

for all intents and purposes	in reference to
the fact of the matter	as a matter of fact
function of	at this point in time
the reason being	due to the fact that
in light of the fact that	has the ability to
it is important that	on the occasion of
at this/that point in time	

Clichés

You may be tempted to use clichés in your writing. Clichés are trite, over-used phrases, which will add no significant content to your ideas.

Quick as a flash, he ran out the door, but he *faced an uphill battle* because a person has to be *young at heart* in today's world in order to *play with fire.* Even though he was *as strong as an ox,* he was *as blind as a bat* when it came to *his pride and joy* and it would have been a *win-win situation* if he had *avoided it like the plague.*

What are those sentences all about? Here are some other common clichés—avoid them "like the plague."

win-win situation	win-lose situation	better late than never
blind as a bat	out like a light	playing with fire
pride and joy	hard as a rock	water under the bridge
in the blink of an eye	easier said than done	avoid . . . like the plague
flat as a pancake	last but not least	never a dull moment
cold as ice	hot as hell	smart as a whip
strong as an ox	in today's world	in this day and age
sly as a fox	green with envy	on easy street

easy as pie	uphill battle	young at heart
quick as a flash	flip side of the coin	slowly but surely

Passive vs. Active Voice

You may be familiar with the squiggly green lines that some word processing software places under words in your documents, perhaps accompanied by a little warning that says "avoid passive voice." What is passive voice?

Examine the picture to the left. When describing the action taking place, we can say

The magician ***pulls*** the rabbit out of the hat.

This is considered **active voice** because the magician is the one performing the action (pulling) and *magician* is in the subject slot of the sentence.

However, what if we want to have *rabbit* in the sentence position, but we still want to use a form of the verb ***pull***. We would have to write

The rabbit ***is pulled*** out of the hat by the magician.

Because the rabbit is doing nothing and is merely the passive recipient of the action being performed, we consider this sentence to be **passive voice.**

Here are some more examples.

- Last night, the Board members voted on the amendment. (active)
- Last night, the amendment was voted on by the Board members. (passive)

- Most students easily passed the final exam. (active)
- The final exam was easily passed by most students. (passive)

- Glass covered the leather seats. (active)
- The seats were covered with glass. (passive)

There will be times when you need to include passive voice in your writing. If, for instance, you have a whole paragraph focused on the damage to an automobile, you may include the sentence

The leather seats were covered with glass.

But avoid too many sentences written in the passive voice.

EXERCISE 13B

DIRECTIONS: Change each of the following sentences from passive to active voice.

1. In the last election, Proposition 11 was voted on.
2. In order to help reduce the cost of tuition, some adjustments to the budget will need to be made.
3. When it started raining during the tennis tournament, the match was cancelled.
4. A thick layer of grease covered my stovetop.
5. Every year, thousands of acres of forests in California are destroyed by wildfires.

Parallel Structures for Lists and Repeated Elements in a Sentence

We all remember nursery rhymes, partly because of the rhyming words but more importantly because of the parallel structures used. Think of "Humpty Dumpty."

> Humpty Dumpty sat on a wall.
> Humpty Dumpty had a great fall.
> All the kings horses,
> And all the kings men,
> Couldn't put Humpty together again.

Now consider the lines "all the kings horses/and all the kings men." Notice the rhythm to these phrases. But what would happen if the lines read as follows?

> All the kings horses,
> And a full complement of the king's soldiers.

It just doesn't have the same effect. The same can be said of the following pairs of sentences.

- I like jogging, hiking, and swimming.
- I like to jog, going hiking, and to go for a swim.

Note the rhythm in the first sentence and how the second one is jarring, the list of "activities" not quite as clear. The reason? Parallel structure. The first sentence presents the list of activities all as *-ing* words; the second one includes an infinitive, a participial phrase, and an infinitive plus prepositional phrase. Whenever you present a list of items, two or more, use the same parts of speech. The list may be words, phrases, or clauses.

- Tom usually eats **apples, oranges,** or **bananas** for snacks. (words)
- At that intersection, cars can turn **to the left** or **to the right**. (phrases)

- After dropping her daughter off at school, Alice drove *to the bank,* *to the post office,* and *to the mall.* (phrases)
- *Samantha likes to drive her car,* but *Conchita prefers to ride her bicycle.* (clauses)

Signal Words

You may have already noticed the use of conjunctions in the above sentences—*or, and, but.* However, there are other words/phrases that indicate the need for parallel elements.

- You should *either* make your bed *or* take a shower.
- *Neither* our nosey neighbor *nor* our friendly mailman noticed that our mailbox was missing.
- College students should *not only* attend class regularly *but also* do assignments promptly.

EXERCISE 13C

DIRECTIONS: Add parallel elements for the *bolded and italicized word(s).*

1. Don't forget to *lock the door,* and _____.
2. When choosing a boyfriend, Juanita always looks for someone who is *honest,* _____, and _____.
3. If you want to lose weight, you should both *eat less* and _____.
4. Neither *Fred's cousin* nor _____ helped him move.
5. Once school is out, I plan to *sleep late,* _____, and _____.

EXERCISE 13D

DIRECTIONS: Make changes in the following sentences to eliminate faulty parallelism.

1. In order to avoid bankruptcy, the airline wanted its employees to either take a pay cut or longer hours working.
2. Without my washing machine, once a week I would have to pack up my clothes, walk several blocks to the Laundromat, and spending several dollars each week.
3. My husband uses the remote control to change channels, entertain himself, and he likes to annoy me.
4. Before class today, I read my math book, typed my English paper, and organizing my binder.
5. My younger sister is always busy but never seeming to get anything done.

CHAPTER 14
Punctuation

COMMAS

The **comma** (,) is the most frequently used punctuation mark. Because it is so frequently used, it is also frequently misused. There are many rules governing the use of commas, and although we will not cover all of them here, the following are the most common uses of the comma:

- **Before a coordinating conjunction *(and, but, or, for, nor, so, yet)* joining two independent clauses.**

    I've looked everywhere, but I can't find my wallet.

    James is a student during the day, and he works at night.

- **Between a dependent clause and an independent clause if the dependent clause comes first in the sentence.**

    Because of the rain, the game has been rescheduled for next Saturday.

    Although I like vegetables, I doubt I could be a vegetarian.

- **After an introductory phrase or clause.**

    By the time I get home, the house must be clean.

    To become a doctor, one must spend many years in school.

- **To set off non-essential information or an expression that interrupts a sentence.**

    What angers me the most, however, is your utter lack of remorse.

    Laziness, according to some, will be the downfall of our society.

- **Between three or more items in a series that are of equal importance.**

In order to pass statistics, you must seek tutoring assistance, attend all class sessions, and spend at least an hour a day studying the material.

Romano, parmesan, and mozzarella are my three favorite cheeses.

**Note: Though you may have learned that the comma before the "and" is optional, it is best to include it to prevent confusion.

- **To set off mild interjections,** *yes* and *no,* **and direct addresses.**

   No, you can't have pizza for breakfast.

   Get your feet off the coffee table, Jim.

   Oh, I didn't realize you were home.

- **Between coordinate adjectives not joined by** *and.*

   Calm, gentle coaxing is the best way to get a cat into its pet carrier for a trip to the vet.

   Yoga is a peaceful, relaxing form of exercise.

- **To set off contrasting expressions and interrogative elements.**

   Greed, not money, is the root of all evil.

   You'll pick me up after work tonight, right?

- **To set off non-restrictive elements (elements that add information but do not change the meaning of the sentence).**

   My best friend, who lives in Santa Cruz, comes to visit me once a month.

   Her car, an SUV, has been stolen twice this year.

- **To set off expressions such as "he said" or "she commented" from direct quotations.**

   "I am tired of listening to this nonsense," he said angrily.

   "One thing you should remember," she said, "is that some people never change."

- **In numbers, addresses, dates, names of places, and informal letters.**

   49, 568

   1425 Olive Street, Anywhere, California 00009

   March 30, 2003

   Sacramento, California

   Dear Grandma and Grandpa,

Using Commas

DIRECTIONS: Insert commas where they are needed in the following sentences. Some sentences may require more than one comma.

1. My favorite subjects in school are English Spanish and psychology.
2. Gary is the tall skinny man standing next to the short chubby one.
3. Unless you pay your bill within three days your phone will be disconnected.
4. My mother warned me about Jake but I refused to listen.
5. Yes the committee will be meeting today at 4:00.
6. How are your parents Lisa?
7. The Monterey Bay Aquarium in Monterey California is a popular destination for tourists.
8. The White House is located at 1600 Pennsylvania Avenue Washington D.C.
9. Bill asked "Who ate the last piece of pizza?"
10. I had a scary realistic dream last night.
11. Jerry is in all honesty one of my least favorite people.
12. John does not enjoy watching sports on T.V. nor does he like attending sporting events.
13. I prefer warm sunny days to cold rainy ones.
14. Because you are my friend I'll lend you money just this once.
15. Meditation exercise and a balanced diet are the keys to good health.

More on Using Commas

DIRECTIONS: Insert commas where they are needed in the following paragraph. Some sentences may require more than one comma.

Volunteering one's time to help others can be a life-altering experience. After graduating from high school I spent the summer working with economically disadvantaged children and I could not believe what a great experience it was. The kids mostly orphans or separated from their parents because of abuse or neglect were eager to have an adult authority figure they could trust and rely on. I read to them played games with them and tutored them in all academic subjects. I took them to movies and sporting events and we even formed our own soccer team. Since most of the children had no parents or had minimal contact with their parents I acted as a combination parent/teacher/friend for them. I quickly became someone they could talk to and have fun with but they understood that I was also in charge of them and that they had to listen to me. It was truly amazing to see shy scared kids turn into happy confident ones over the course of that summer. The experience was a period of tremendous growth for me as well for I learned the joy of selflessly giving of my time and energy to help others. Since that summer I have also volunteered my time in teaching adults to read tutoring high school kids in English and serving meals to the homeless on Thanksgiving and Christmas. Overall my experiences as a volunteer have molded me into a person who seeks out opportunities to help my fellow human beings and for this I am truly grateful.

OTHER PUNCTUATION MARKS

Semicolons

The **semicolon** (;) is a versatile but frequently misused punctuation mark. Here some common uses of the semicolon:

- **Between two independent clauses that are closely related but NOT joined by a coordinating conjunction.**
  - Your friends are not mind-readers; you can't expect them to know when you need to hear from them.
  - It's a shame that Gary got laid off from his job; he was a really hard worker.

- **Between two related independent clauses joined by a conjunctive adverb** *(therefore, however, thus, consequently, etc.)*
  - My alarm clock didn't go off this morning; consequently, I was late for class.
  - You didn't finish your homework; therefore, you can't watch television tonight.

- **Between items in a series, if the items contain internal punctuation.**
  - The most self-sufficient and trouble-free of all pets, cats require very little training; need a minimum of grooming, entertainment, and supervision; and can virtually care for themselves.
  - When I went to the grocery store, I purchased milk, 2%; cheese, Wisconsin cheddar; and a pork roast, cooked, sliced, and ready to eat.

**Note: Do not use a semicolon between a dependent clause and an independent clause or to introduce a list.

- When I had finished my homework; I watched television.
- Francisca had three jobs this semester; McDonalds, Round Table, and Steve's Pizza.

Colons

The **colon (:)** is also a very versatile punctuation mark, and like the semicolon, it is often misused. Note that the semicolon and colon are used in very different ways and that, generally, they are not interchangeable.

Here are the most common uses of the colon:

- **Between two independent clauses if the second one explains or re-states the first:**

    Pets are like children: They need a lot of love and attention.

- **To call attention to a list, a direct quotation, or an appositive.**
    - **A list:**
        A good daily health regimen should include the following: well-balanced meals, a vitamin supplement, plenty of liquids, and at least 30 minutes of vigorous exercise.

    - **An appositive:**
        I am making a sincere effort to break my two worst habits: fidgeting and nail-biting.

    - **A direct quotation:**
        My grandfather gave me only one piece of advice while he was alive: "Know as much as possible about your friends, and know even more about your enemies."

- **After the greeting in a letter, between a title and a subtitle, in ratios, and in expressions of time.**
    - To Whom It May Concern:
    - One of Henry James' most famous stories is *Daisy Miller: A Study.*
    - The ratio of desserts to entrees was 3:1.
    - The luncheon will begin at 11:30 a.m.

**Note: Do not use a colon to introduce a list preceded by a verb, after the transitions "for example," "for instance," and "such as," or between a preposition and its object. All of the following are INCORRECT:

- The most important things you need to remember to bring are: hiking shoes, a flashlight, and bottled water.
- The Shakespearean sonnet consists of: three quatrains and a couplet.
- Annabelle has been to many exotic places for example: Paris, Milan, and Munich.

EXERCISE 14B

Semicolons vs. Colons

DIRECTIONS: Each of the following sentences needs either a semicolon OR a colon. Insert the correct punctuation where it is needed (Note: You may also need to add commas and/or capital letters, depending on the sentence).

1. Love is like air we take it for granted but then miss it when it is gone.
2. John doesn't realize the impact his actions have on others consequently he is surprised when people respond negatively to him.
3. Terry needs more practice on two important aspects of driving starting and stopping.
4. My mother frequently repeated these words of wisdom "Pretty is as pretty does."
5. To be a good pet owner, one must be able to provide all of the following fresh food and water, a safe environment, and an abundance of love.
6. My alarm clock didn't go off this morning therefore I missed my first class.
7. It is a good idea to do favors for others you never know when you may need to ask for a favor in return.
8. One of the most important rules of life is also one of the simplest you get what you give.
9. The class consists of a diverse group of students including Josh, who is still in high school Rita, who has five grandchildren and Maiko, who just arrived in the U.S. from Japan.
10. Sacramento's wide variety of trees includes the following the Coast Live Oak, the Giant Sequoia, the Liquid Amber, and the Valencia Orange.

Dashes

The **dash** (—) is used when a stronger break than a comma is needed and particularly when you want something to stand out. The dash is typed as two hyphens with no space before or after them (--). Most word processing software will then join and elongate the two hyphens to form a dash (—).

Here are the most common uses of the dash.

- To indicate a sudden change in sentence construction or an abrupt break in thought.

  The table was an antique—as if he cared.

- After an introductory list. The words *these, those, all,* and occasionally *such* introduce the part after the dash.

  Apples, oranges, grapefruit, pears—these are the fruits I like best.

  Picnics, baseball games, lazy afternoons by the river—such are my memories of my childhood summers.

- To set off material that interrupts the flow of an idea, that needs emphasis, or that restates an idea as an appositive.

  You are—I am certain—not serious. (interrupting)

  Our next question is—how much money did we raise? (emphasis)

  My mother—the best cook in the world—baked an apple pie yesterday. (appositive)

- To indicate an interruption or an unfinished statement, often in dialogue.

  Jason sulkily replied, "I only wanted to—" (no period)

  "Shall we—" Fred asked. (no comma)

**Do not use a dash in places in which other punctuation marks would be more appropriate.

Not	Susan went to the beach—and she went swimming.
But	Susan went to the beach, and she went swimming.

Apostrophes

The **apostrophe** (') is used in the following instances:

- **To indicate the omission of letters in a contraction.** Contractions are words made of two words joined together (will not = won't, cannot=can't, it is=it's, etc.) The apostrophe must be placed where the omitted letters would have been.
  - I haven't been to Disneyland this year.
  - He doesn't understand why your feelings are hurt.
  - We won't be on time if you don't hurry!

- **To indicate that a noun or indefinite pronoun (*anyone, someone, no one, everyone, etc.*) is possessive.** Apostrophes are added to indicate ownership—that something *belongs to* someone or something.
  - The car belonging to Janice = *Janice's* car
  - The book belonging to the student= the *student's* book
  - The responsibility of everyone=*everyone's* responsibility

**Note that if the noun does not end in "s," it must be added.

If a noun is singular and already ends in "s," you may add another "s" unless it would make pronunciation of the word awkward or difficult.

- James' breakfast (or James's breakfast)

If the noun is plural and already ends in "s," the apostrophe must go after the "s."

- The boys' bicycles
- The students' desks

- **To pluralize abbreviations, numbers mentioned as numbers, letters mentioned as letters, and words mentioned as words.**
  - When we got to the door of the club, the host asked us to show him our I.D.'s.
  - There are five 4's in my phone number.
  - The teacher told us that she gave only two A's on the essay.
  - Larry is the classic doormat; all his answers are yes's.

**Note: Do NOT use apostrophes in plural nouns that are not possessive or in the possessive pronouns (*his, hers, its, theirs, ours, whose,* and *yours*)

EXERCISE 14C

Using Apostrophes Correctly

DIRECTIONS: Each of the following sentences needs at least ONE apostrophe (some need more than one). Insert apostrophes where needed.

1. Grading stacks of essays is all in a days work for an English teacher.
2. The recent budget cuts are not in the students best interests.
3. When the air is badly polluted, everyones quality of life suffers.
4. When Sharon broke up with her boyfriend, he called her constantly, inundating her with whys.
5. The grading breakdown on the exam was three As, six Bs, eight Cs, and no Ds or Fs.
6. I dont know whose car that is, but it must be moved immediately.
7. My high school class fifteenth reunion is coming up next year.
8. Its not enough to simply recycle aluminum cans; we must recycle glass, paper, and plastic as well.
9. When I was a child, my parents rules always seemed strict to me, but now that Im an adult, I understand why they enforced those rules.
10. Californias crime statistics for this year are expected to be lower than last years.

Quotation Marks

Quotation marks (" ") are used in the following instances:

- **To indicate a direct quotation from a speaker or a writer.** The quotation marks serve to "enclose" the quotation so that the reader can tell where the quotation begins and ends.
  - The *Declaration of Independence* guarantees the right of every person to "life, liberty, and the pursuit of happiness."
  - As I walked out the door, my mother asked, "Where are you going?"
  - "I left my keys in the restaurant," Kelly said.

**Note: End punctuation must be placed inside the quotation marks when directly quoting another's words.

- **To enclose the title of an essay, article, short story, short poem, or other short works of literature.**
  - "Easter 1916" is one of my favorite poems.
  - One of F. Scott Fitzgerald's most famous stories is "Babylon Revisited."

EXERCISE 14D

Using Quotation Marks Correctly

DIRECTIONS: Insert quotation marks as needed in the following sentences.

1. My grandmother, the eternal optimist, always said, every cloud has a silver lining.
2. I'm afraid, John said, that your apology is not accepted.
3. One of my favorite sayings is the best things in life are free.
4. The Tell-Tale Heart is one of Edgar Allan Poe's most popular stories.
5. The remote control is gone again, Frank complained. It was just here a minute ago.
6. When I was a child, my favorite story was The Princess and the Pea.
7. Where are you taking me for dinner? Suzanne asked.
8. Joshua argued, But the dog really *did* eat my homework!
9. Next time, my English teacher told me, be sure to turn your essay in on time.
10. Today, the class analyzed Matthew Arnold's famous poem Dover Beach.

EXERCISE 14E

Review: Other Punctuation Marks

DIRECTIONS: The following paragraphs are missing colons, semi-colons, dashes, apostrophes, and quotation marks. Insert the various punctuation marks where needed.

The world is a vastly different place than it was when I was a kid. Granted, times have to change however, things seem to have changed drastically in the last fifteen years or so. These changes have been much like earthquakes they have been entirely unexpected and have done some serious damage. One of these changes is the boom in technology of the latter half of the twentieth century. Its amazing what has been done with computers in the last several decades they have gone from being huge, cumbersome machines to portable, efficient devices that can be used at home, at work, at school, and even at the local coffee shop. The astronomical increase in the use of computers has its positive effects however, there are many negatives as well. One of these negatives is the drastic increase in the occurrence of identity theft. Peoples identities are being stolen far more frequently than ever before, and its largely due to the easy access to others personal information, including names, addresses, social security numbers and credit card numbers. Internet-related identity theft has caused much damage to many peoples credit ratings and lives.

Technology has also drastically depersonalized our society. Computers have taken the place of humans at many businesses consequently, when we call a particular company, such as a bank, it is rare that we actually get to speak to a real person. This can be problematic a computer might not be able to answer specific questions we might have or fix a problem that has arisen. Moreover, the lack of human contact may lead to some very negative emotions frustration and anger. In addition, if a computer makes a mistake, its more difficult for the customer to hold anyone accountable for the mistake because its nearly impossible to place blame on an inanimate object.

Advances in technology have not only caused a great deal of negative emotion theyve also put lives in danger. The rise in popularity of cell phones has led many drivers to spend a lot of time on their cell phones while driving as a result, car accidents due to driver inattention have nearly doubled in the last few years. In addition to phones, yet another technological advance now presents a safety hazard on the roadways the car television. Initially intended to keep children occupied in the backseats of minivans, televisions are now found in the dashboard consoles of all kinds of vehicles, often in the drivers direct line of vision. One can only imagine the level of distraction that could result when drivers take their eyes off the road to catch the five o'clock news or <u>Wheel of Fortune</u>.

I realize that technology is not all bad, and I hope I dont sound like my father, whose constant lament is the world goes further downhill with every passing year. I do, however, often find myself longing for the simpler days when my identity couldnt be stolen with the click of a computer mouse and when drivers paid attention to the road rather than a T.V. show or a heated phone conversation.

Index